Sydney Smith.

Jr

C

onlince.

CAMBRIDGE AND CLARE

Clare Old Court, from the Backs, under light snow

CAMBRIDGE & CLARE

SIR HARRY GODWIN F.R.S.

FELLOW OF CLARE COLLEGE,
EMERITUS PROFESSOR OF BOTANY,
UNIVERSITY OF CAMBRIDGE

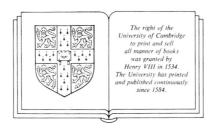

The right of the
University of Cambridge
to print and sell
all manner of books
was granted by
Henry VIII in 1534.
The University has printed
and published continuously
since 1584.

CAMBRIDGE UNIVERSITY PRESS

CAMBRIDGE

LONDON   NEW YORK   NEW ROCHELLE
MELBOURNE   SYDNEY

Published by the Press Syndicate of the University of Cambridge
The Pitt Building, Trumpington Street, Cambridge CB2 1RP
32 East 57th Street, New York, NY 10022, USA
10 Stamford Road, Oakleigh, Melbourne, 3166, Australia

First published 1985

Printed in Great Britain by
the University Press, Cambridge

Library of Congress catalogue card number: 85-3780

British Library cataloguing in publication data
Godwin, Sir Harry
Cambridge and Clare.
1. Clare College, Cambridge – History
I. Title
378.426'59'09   LF155
ISBN 0 521 30765 1

CONTENTS

ILLUSTRATIONS

ILLUSTRATIONS

ILLUSTRATIONS

ILLUSTRATIONS

ILLUSTRATIONS

PREFACE

Sɪxᴛʏ-ᴏᴅᴅ ʏᴇᴀʀs in residence have given me a close-up view of tremendous changes in the structure and quality of both collegiate and university life, so that without any pretensions to exact historical record or appraisal, one's memories reflect the altering circumstances and the shape of societies now largely displaced. Aside from the modification of the whole of British society, Cambridge itself underwent at least four major evolutionary advances. The first, begun just before the turn of the century, was the extension to all college fellows of the right to retain fellowship status after marriage. This provision had the massive social consequence of removing the exclusive, almost divine, right of heads of houses to constitute with their wives a society beyond the common herd. It naturally followed that the dons and their wives now practised for themselves a meticulous code of calling, dining, gossiping and co-existing. This society in its turn fell into decay as a consequence of the First World War and my wife and I, married in 1927, were in time to experience only its ultimate decay.

The second great evolutionary advance within the university arose from bringing into effect, directly after the First World War, the proposals of the Royal Commission on the Universities of Oxford and Cambridge. New statutes now altered the whole structural relationship of university and colleges, which took on a fresh and singularly democratic administrative quality that happily still persists.

No comparable third evolutionary step occurred until, in the late 1940s, the government of the day vastly extended the financing of university education and in so doing provided Oxbridge colleges with fees and maintenance for all qualified students, so that all colleges were now assured of filling a full complement of places, and could confidently embark upon deserving but long-delayed plans for improvement. This represented a vast change in circumstances for many of the poorer and less-populated colleges and their fellows no longer had to await the annual audit to discover whether to expect a dividend or to have to help the college from their own pockets.

Moreover, as in this new regime the weight of university teaching was largely sustained by money coming from the University Grants Committee, the members of university teaching posts were greatly augmented, so permitting great expansion in the size of college fellowship bodies, in Clare from a dozen or so in 1920 to over fifty at the present day. Furthermore, not only is the undergraduate intake now less preponderantly drawn from the public schools but so too, inevitably, are the college fellowship and university administration.

Into the adventure of the fourth evolutionary advance in college and university life we are as yet barely launched. It was as late as 1970 that King's, Clare and Churchill colleges were committed to adopt co-residence of women students, a move subsequently repeated by almost all the Cambridge colleges. At undergraduate level the new dispositions have been extremely effective and popular but so far women are only lightly represented in the senior ranks of college and university and one feels oneself too close to judge where the new evolutionary process will lead.

Looking back across my own experience of Cambridge life it seems apparent that it is the earliest phases that will be most likely to command interest, if only because witnesses of them are now grown scarce. Accordingly I write very little of events since 1960, a convention that fits pretty well with my intention, (which contains also a measure of self-preservation) not to refer, save very exceptionally and shortly, to colleagues who are still living and playing their part in managing college and university affairs.

The science don in Cambridge exhibits in strong degree a duality of concern and loyalty, for whilst affection and local ties

PREFACE

bind him closely to his college, he cannot hope to succeed as a scientist unless he becomes intensely committed to both teaching and research, which must in the nature of things, carry him into university laboratories and lecture-rooms and draw him into close contact with scientific colleagues from other colleges, indeed of other universities and countries. Since to some extent my account must reflect my own profession and scientific progress, it must naturally carry a substantial botanical flavour and have to do with the Botany School and those scientific colleagues of its staff from whom one drew instruction and support.

This book, so hard to entitle, can perhaps best be taken as an offering to the many devotees on the one hand, of Flora, and on the other of 'Aula cara', the foundation of Elizabetha de Clare.

H. G.

Cambridge
October 1984

ACKNOWLEDGEMENTS

THROUGHOUT the years of my academic life my experience has consistently been that of such generous assistance that this book might well have had for sub-title 'The ubiquitous helpfulness of scholars', and I trust that the reader will be assured how constantly I have been aware of my debt to innumerable friends and colleagues mostly unnamed in the text.

A special compulsion is nevertheless upon me to acknowledge help in the particular circumstances that evoked the writing and permitted the publication of this volume. It originated from the kindness of the Master and Fellows of Clare College in marking my eightieth birthday by giving Margaret, my wife, and myself a celebratory dinner in the College Hall, where gaiety and goodwill combined to provoke from me a reminiscent message of thanks, not only to the present fellowship, but to the former fellows, staff and students who had so effectively built up the tradition and reputation that the college now enjoys. I evoked, as far as I was able, the image of a former college society now slipping beyond recollection. So instant was the appeal of this call upon interest and affection that I was immediately and pressingly begged to have printed the gist of my talk, which was supposed (quite wrongly) to be somewhere written down and secreted upon my person. The enthusiasm and variety of encouragement received led to two years of rewarding though frequently nostalgic recapture and organisation of my recollections. In this task, more demanding than might at first be supposed, I had outstanding help from several sources.

For the representation of the rich architectural and environmental charm of Clare, we were able to take advantage of the tremendous labours of Mansfield Forbes in compiling the great two-volume book commemorative of the college sexcentenary.

xix

Forbes had not only commissioned special artists such as Sydney S. Carline and J. F. Greenwood to undertake individual *ad hoc* representations, but had engaged the special interest of leading periodicals to focus particular attention upon the college and its gardens. Forbes's own diligence and aesthetic perception ensured a record at once pleasurable and authentic, more especially by his introduction of the *Country Life* photographers to his own favourite vantage spots. Their superb pictures appeared in the *Book of Clare* and are reproduced here: the reader may judge of their quality by their rendering of the enchantment of the college 'roof-scapes'. I am also grateful for photographs taken by *Amateur Gardening*, Heffers Printers Ltd., Mr W. H. Palmer, Professor R. G. West and, from the 1949 issue of the college magazine, Angus Arnold Thomas.

The *Lady Clare* has been a rich source both of collegiate recollection and of appropriate illustration, extending as far back as the days of my own undergraduate editorship in the early 1920s. Contributors thus originating have been mentioned individually in the printed captions where the names are still available, but I nevertheless acknowledge separately such outstanding artists as C. F. Millett and Raymond McGrath. Original works of portraiture have been individually acknowledged but here and there one does not know who drew some especially telling picture.

As, over fifty years ago, I sought the help of the Cambridge University Press in publication of my *Plant Biology*, so I have been privileged to draw upon the experience of the same press in production of this present work, most especially for the courtesy and competence of Dr Alan Winter, Director of the American Branch and Mr Michael H. Black, the University Publisher.

In consequence of my dual linkage with Clare College on the one hand and the University Department of Botany on the other, I have finally the pleasant task of thanking the Master, Bursar and the college staffs that they direct, for much freely given help with searching, typing and duplicating, whilst I readily acknowledge a similar debt to Professor R. G. West F.R.S., Head of the Botany School and his uniformly helpful colleagues and staff.

Honesty and pride compel me to conclude that my heart-felt gratitude rests with my wife, Margaret, who has, these many years, tolerantly and sympathetically favoured all my more reputable activities.

I
SCHOOL

I WAS BORN IN ROTHERHAM, South Yorkshire, in a small house where at night the rooms were vividly lit by the glare of the Bessemer steel converters. Of this I have no recollection, for when I was only a few months old, my parents moved to the growing township of Long Eaton, actually within South Derbyshire though outside the limits of the South Derbyshire coalfield and substantially closer and more in touch with Nottingham than with the county town. My father, a young grocer and licensed victualler, was taking advantage of the considerable local development of railway siding and associated wagon building alongside a great Nottingham-centred expansion of the machine making of lace.

A community of this expansive character was highly eligible to profit from the Parliament Act of 1870 by which, in areas that could not provide for all the local children of school age, 'Board Schools' might be publicly provided. Despite some opposition from the established church schools, the 'High Street Board School' had thus been opened in 1876 and this is where I attended school in the 'Infants', at the age of three or four. It was a daunting brick and stone Victorian building, and set in the yard alongside was a detached house that always puzzled me, for its symmetrical upper floor with oval table and surrounding chairs was given over merely to the infrequent meetings of the board, whilst the lower floor was the office of the attendance officer, a sad Dickensian figure, known to us as 'the kid-hunter', a man whose function was to visit parents and enquire into the too long or too frequent absences of their offspring from school.

After transit through the 'Boys', at the age of twelve I exchanged the Board School with its atmosphere of corduroy

S. Clegg; headmaster of the utmost distinction

trousers and heavy boots as worn by all my friends, for the wider territory of a progressive new school, drawing its pupils from a radius of several miles. This was the County School and Pupil–Teacher Centre opened in 1910 with Samuel Clegg as headmaster and conducted upon lines advocated by Michael Sadler the outstanding educational theorist of the opening twentieth century and, specifically, consultant to the Derbyshire County Council upon secondary and higher education. The placing of particular emphasis upon drawing and artistic appreciation was visualised as suitable to the staple lace-making industry of the town, and it could not have been placed in more enthusiastic or more competent hands than those of the new headmaster. To begin with, Mr Clegg had the ear of the County Surveyor, G. W. Widdows, who was responsible for the design of a delightful modern building remarkable for many important features, not least a central, spacious 'Art Room', providing a north-lighted studio that became the heart of Clegg's curricula of those courses in drawing and design that were applied throughout the school, taking up a large proportionate measure of school time. The aims and achievements of this pioneering enterprise were effectively publicised by the book that Clegg afterwards published.

I did not advance to the 'Pupil-Teacher Centre' as a result of sitting for a scholarship, and indeed at this age had no idea of such mechanisms; but my parents having seen the head, I became a fee-paying student, although a 'Free Place', value £1 per annum, one of several at the disposal of the headmaster, was found for me within a term or two of admission. Even now I recall with vividness how impressed I was in my new environment by a style of teaching hitherto new to me: I recall returning home at lunch-time and trying to explain this amazing experience. Instead of receiving *ex cathedra* a piece of information (as hitherto), we were actually 'invited' to consider the reasons for each conclusion which might be drawn, and indeed were expected to say if the steps in the argument were not quite clear. No doubt it was elementary mathematics or simple physics that we dealt with, but whatever the subject the effect on me was dramatic and I remember feeling (and announcing) that this was indeed *my* sort of school. Nor had I reason later on to think myself mistaken in this assessment. My good fortune was actually far greater than I knew, for Samuel Clegg was a teacher and head of altogether exceptional quality, by whom it was my good fortune to be fostered and encouraged right through school and into university life. He had cut short his own university career at Owen's College, Manchester, after the two years needed for a teaching certificate, turning directly to begin elementary school teaching. This course took him to several of the Long Eaton schools then undergoing modification in structure and grading: the progressive young teacher remained in the van of these changes in the local educational system so that in 1910 he became headmaster of the newly built County School, an organisation still embracing the Pupil-Teacher's Centre at which Samuel Clegg had already demonstrated his gifts as teacher and organiser.

The achievements of the new head through the next twenty years were altogether outstanding both in civic sociological terms and in those of educational progress. Now, fifty years since his death, I still find it impossible to account for the breadth, imagination and incisiveness of his mind except as the product of a natural swift eruption of a genius for learning and the gift of perceiving how best to develop love of learning and culture in young people. A biologist thinks of hidden genes suddenly found in harmonious contiguity and suitable environment. Some suggestion of the same assemblage can be seen in the personality of his grandson, the much-respected biologist, David Attenborough.

I trust it may go at least a small distance in conveying the nature of the school that Sam brought into being if I give a notion of some of its attributes, especially those associated with the teaching of visual art, as they appealed to a boy in his commencing teens.

As a beginning the headmaster, with deliberate intention, made of his new school a beautiful environment kept meticulously clean and unspoiled. The parquet floors of corridors and class rooms, the stained wooden panelling and pictures were each morning swept and dusted throughout, a task simplified by the absence of graphs, maps, timetable and general clutter from the walls. No thumb-tacks or ugly holes from them sullied the surface, so that defacement was unthinkable, the more reasonably so in view of Sam's tremendous care to select for each class room its own particular set of high-grade pictures upon one unifying theme, each picture given the attention of its appropriate framing, possibly by reconstruction of wood and gesso copies of originals from the school woodwork shop. Above the panelling stretched five feet or so of a continuous fresco, that in many of the rooms had been decorated, almost one might say 'illuminated', by a coordinated mural painting by some visiting artist happy to cooperate. The flat tempera of the 'Chaucer Room' exhibited the linear progress of the well-loved Pilgrims; another displayed typical scenes of work in the local lace factories, and yet another had been painted by Mlle Rosa Vaerwyck, once Professor of Figure-Painting at Ghent and now expressing nostalgic affection from the Flanders countryside as she remembered it free from the defilement of war. It was Rosa Vaerwyck who also carried through the decoration of the Elizabethan room and allowed some senior pupils the dizzy experience of filling in for her the running backcloth of Tudor gardens and hedges. It was she also, with fellow refugees from Belgium, who introduced into our language classes a stream of relatives of miscellaneous size, age, shape and vocalisation, for conversation and 'dictées', so enlarging our familiarity with spoken French that at the ensuing Oxford Local Examinations, the class was awarded, throughout, distinction in the spoken language.

Art instruction was a constant joy to me and I believe to a great many pupils, particularly because it was the head's own especial care and the vehicle of his own particular sensitivity. The field of study varied extensively: one week we might proceed via studies of a growing plant into designs suitable for borders in colour or line, the next to patterns of space-filling as shown by intervals and breadths of framing, next to oriental carpet design, or copying butterfly colouration as a clue to colour contrast and combination, and the setting of borders on the curved surface of cups or plates. Some of the studies produced designs for embroidery put into effect by the girls' needlework, or into coloured wood-block printing evolved by Sam as a simplification of the traditional Japanese technique by which both cutting and printing were effected in the school workshop. It was a longer but still pleasurable process that took some, girls as well as boys, from the printed sections of a book to the delight of a properly bound book finally with its own lettering and gilding. Enamelling and wood-carving, like book binding, tended to be for the more experienced few, but practically everyone in the school was introduced to lettering in its various stages and very much use was made of the methods of hand-writing then being so successfully brought into general notice by Edward Johnston.

From mastering the primary alphabets one progressed to the laying out of fine writing, aided by being shown a few consumate originals and by exercises in illumination and the design of capital letters with and without colour or gilding. Sam insisted that our efforts be directed always to some prose or poetry worth the craftsman's effort and some pupils brought great aptitude and sensitiveness to their efforts so that it is not too much to say that in almost all of us there was implanted a lasting awareness of those virtues of fine printing that have the potential so much to enhance the contemporary scene.

Whatever the type of art exercise on which we were employed, at the well-calculated moment Sam would provide for us, from his own private resources, choice examples of fine products of other times and places, prints, coins, tapestry, lace or manuscript. My mind still vividly recalls thus seeing for the first time that perfection of Greek coinage, the tetradrachm of Syracuse, its head of Ceres serenely encircled by lazy dolphins. Sam seems unlikely to have been at all well-provided for this role, but entirely against the odds of an ill-paid provincial teaching post, all through the years he made weekly train journeys to London to edit the fine-art and collectors' magazine, the *Bibliophile*, through which he kept closely in contact with the art and letters of the metropolis, the vital authors, craftsmen, publishers and galleries of the contemporary scene. The home town of Long Eaton to which he returned had grown up during the previous half-century from a rural village, the railway and the lace industries having attracted a rootless population of nearly 20,000 with little in common save initiative, working-class determination and strong adherence to the numerous non-conformist sects represented locally. Aesthetically and culturally the social landscape was vacant territory for Sam's enthusiasm and his influence on the parochialism of this evolving township over the years was very great. So pronounced had this proved to be that, no more than twenty years after the school had opened, I found on return visits to the town that I could, merely from the outside appearance of houses, their window-hangings, furnishing and decoration, recognise the homes of former pupils at Sam Clegg's school.

What qualities or advantages Mr Clegg himself claimed for the strong emphasis upon teaching art so extensively and devotedly emerges clearly enough from his book *Drawing and Design: a School Course in Composition*, published by I. Pitman in 1918 under a foreword from Professor William Rothenstein. It was not so much a studied exposition of principles as the record of an actual three-year curriculum illustrated freely by the drawings, prints and designs of average pupils taking the course: nonetheless the educational philosophy of the author emerges with force and clarity.

The emphasis on visual aesthetics had a particular value in my particular case, realised only as my own scientific interests declared themselves. As soon as biologists had adopted T. H. Huxley's principle of teaching by direct examination of plant and animal material in the laboratory, the admirable practice established itself of recording all observations by careful draw-ings, properly labelled and annotated. The interplay of inspec-tion and of execution of the record was powerful in either direction, as Sam Clegg was well aware, and I never found it hard to accept the axiom of that admirable Japanese painter, Hokusai, who held that 'one picture tells more than a thousand words'. In the environment of Sam Clegg's school it was unsurprising that, encouraged by an able teacher of botany, I devoted much effort to botanical drawing, and learned a great deal from the considerable variety of material that I surveyed, often with no great anxiety whether scientific or aesthetic ends were being served. In my later school days I somehow acquired a copy of that monumental volume created by the Oxford botanist, A. H. Church. Entitled *Types of Floral Mechanism*, it was lavishly strewn with coloured and monochrome plates of impeccable accuracy, that displayed the structure and precise organisation of flowers, bulbs and other stem structures involved in plant reproduction. After directly copying one or two of these plates I went on to make similar large coloured illustrations of the flowers of many other species and organs, including the sordid, squat purplish-umber urn-shaped flowers of the *Aspidistra*, that are to be found now and then on the soil-surface where, one is told, they are attractive to the beetles or snails that effect pollination. When I became, at a later date, a demonstrator in the Cambridge Botany School, I found that extremely few students had received even the most elementary of drawing lessons, and most were able to benefit at once by even very simple devices for 'setting-out' any representation called for in their records.

The establishment of the new secondary school faced not only social difficulties in the acceptance of new ideas and ideals, but most of all in the hardships of recruiting and maintaining staff through the rigours of the First World War. With almost all the male staff absent on national service, senior pupils took over many day-to-day duties of running the school, but serious gaps persisted in the teaching of many subjects, especially mathematics and the physical sciences. There was no doubt a measure of compensating advantage in that pupils were forced back on their own resources for reading and experiment. The senior boys in my own form made grateful use for their 'homework' of the facilities of the public library adjacent to the school and stocked with such delectable material as the annual reports of the Carnegie Institute of Washington, a consequence of the original Carnegie bequest of the Library to the town. My own indebtedness was outstandingly to a purchase of the two massive volumes of Kerner and Oliver's *Natural History of Plants*, a work overflowing with fascinating botanical information. As I later realised, its outlook was entirely teleological, every structure and mechanism being described in terms of argument from design, 'devices for this purpose', 'structures intended to secure this or that end', and so forth. In the astringent air of the Cambridge Botanical Department, I afterwards shed this philosophy easily enough, whilst happily recollecting the wealth of factual phenomena presented by the two authors. I suppose it must have been from this work that I first realised the interest of plant ecology, at that time scarcely acknowledged, although Kerner had already worked on the vegetation of the Danube valley in central Europe, whilst Oliver was the earliest of the pioneer ecologists who taught in University College London. Whatever the source, I found myself describing for the school magazine the strong floristic contrasts to be seen between the Lower Liassic Limestone outliers on the hills south of the River Trent and the Keuper Marl soils with which they are surrounded. My interest must have been apparent to Mr Clegg, for when the time came to consider my pre-scholarship programme, he announced to me that since I was interested in ecology, common sense suggested that I begin the study of geology, and he added that he had just appointed (as geography teacher) a first-class Birmingham graduate in geology who might well supervise my work in this subject. Thus I followed the course, unusual at that time, of offering geology in the Cambridge entrance scholarship examination, and I began a life-long association with geology in all the manifold interactions that subsist between that subject and botany, not least of which has been ecology itself.

It was as I became senior in the school that I understood how

Mr Clegg's affection for the visual arts was fully matched or exceeded by his love for the English language, its superb legacy of poetry and prose, and those inherent qualities of flexibility and strength that have given it such overwhelming importance to the world. He himself wrote excellently well and undertook a good measure of the teaching of English in the upper forms, where I enjoyed his instruction right to the end of my school career. He taught me much about editing and I did not scruple to draw on his help to overlook the proofs of my earliest book written and published in 1929. There is little doubt in my mind that had he followed a university career, English would have been his preferred academic field. It was his instruction of F. L. Attenborough in that subject at the Pupil-Teacher Centre which took that gifted pupil to the university where, ignoring Sam's advice to try for Cambridge, he successfully applied for entry to Bangor. No sooner there than 'Fred' acknowledged heart-brokenly that he already knew more English than did his new teachers. The repair of this error is another story, but part of it was his return as teacher in the new Long Eaton school where we had every opportunity of profiting from his remarkable gifts as a teacher and his own vital personality. The rapport with his own form was dramatic and I recall an occasion when he was urging us to resume a scripture lesson by saying, 'Remember, the two most important things in life are Scripture and football'; a spontaneous roar from the class instantly amended this to 'Football and scripture', a nice acknowledgement of Fred's own amateur international soccer trial. After this outburst we happily began the scripture class.

Mr Clegg's unsparing services to his early pupil-teachers are illustrated by the way in which he helped to launch the education of another local boy, then acting as railway clerk on the Erewash valley line. Sam would go up the line in the evening to sit with the young Will Bullock, and coach him in the slack intervals of the ticket office. This was Will Bullock who in due course became gold medallist of the Edinburgh medical school and achieved great distinction through and after the First World War, later under the changed surname of Gye.

There can be small wonder at the affection as well as respect with which Samuel Clegg was locally regarded.

II
ENTRY TO CAMBRIDGE

THE LATTER PART of the First World War was a period of
great national harshness and austerity during which the
country's food supplies were at one time so reduced by U-boat
warfare that a reserve for only a few days remained. The ghastly
attrition of trench warfare was reflected in the length of the
queues formed daily at the local post office, where wives and
sweethearts scanned the casualty lists of the local regiments: the
mere absence of mention was a blessing, as was the relief of
reading the message, subsequently blurred with time, 'All quiet
on the Western front'. Many in the queue were seizing the
chance to post parcels of food, chocolate, fags and knitted
comforts, and the general sadness and anxiety were tangible.

Those of my friends able to proceed from school to university
training mostly went daily to Nottingham and it was from them
that I gathered something of the standards and character of the
courses for degrees, in this case aimed at external examinations
of London University. Now and again a group of us attended
an evening lecture in Nottingham and I recall cycling home in
the middle of an air-raid alarm, meeting delivery drays with
horses being galloped home in the darkness. I remember also
how apprehensive we were at having to cross the bridge over
the railway exit to the vast shell-filling factory that had been
built at Chilwell, a mile or so short of our home town. There
was indeed cause for apprehension, for not only on that
occasion did we hear (as we thought) the roar of the approaching
German Gotha aircraft, but we knew the considerable risks that
the factory sustained. I had been at home on the evening of 1
July 1918 when an explosion wrecked the greater part of the
establishment, and had seen the immense cloud of debris and
smoke flowering in the sky and yielding from its summit such

unlikely objects as locomotives, girders and rails that hung for a while before turning down again earthwards. The shell-filling operatives, clad only in overalls, now stumbled, dazed and blackened through the town, revived on their way by house-holders at the doorways, whilst those more seriously hurt were transported by ambulance to established or improvised hospi-tals, and not a few casualties lay upon the characteristically blackened bags of lace that lorries chanced to be bringing back from Nottingham. It says much for the war-time energy of the nation (and likewise for the insatiable lust of the front for ammunition) that the sheds of the rebuilt factory by the time of the Armistice in November again housed over a million filled shells.

By November 1918 I was seventeen and a half years old and due to take the Cambridge College scholarship examinations held a month later. My college preference had been determined by experts. By about the middle of the war, F. L. Attenborough, exempt by a football injury from military service, had saved enough from his stipend as teacher in Mr Clegg's school, to take him to Emmanuel College, Cambridge, there to recommence his university education. Success in the Modern and Medieval Languages Tripos, then the channel for all instruction in English, was followed by undertaking to give college instruction and by acceptance as research student by H. M. Chadwick, holder of the University Chair of Anglo-Saxon. Among Fred Attenborough's close friends was now Mansfield D. Forbes, like Chadwick a Fellow of Clare. 'Manny' was passionately interested in the visual arts and their encouragement in Cambridge, and it was natural that he should be very responsive to the educational views of Mr Clegg as retailed to him by Fred. Thus when the matter of application for entrance to a college came to be decided, it was through Manny and Fred jointly that I received the advice to apply to one of the smaller colleges, such as Clare, it being rightly supposed that I should be more at home there than in the wider acres of say Trinity or St John's. When the scholarship examinations were over and the

H. M. Chadwick, posthumous drawing by Brian Hope-Taylor, 1970

Governing Body had made its awards, it was Manny who had the kindness to telegraph the news of my £60 award, and when I came up in 1919 and thenceforward to his death in 1936, he always offered me great kindness and contributed an invaluable link between the scientist and the lively Cambridge activities of the English School, the contemporary arts and all the vital activities of the humanities of which Manny was part.

I had a brisker reception on my first free afternoon during the scholarship examinations. Invited to tea with Fred Attenborough in the front court rooms of H. S. Bennett in Emmanuel, my host said he supposed I had come up to take the scholarship examinations: upon my admission of it, he said he had imagined so because 'the streets were full of raw callow youths'. This no doubt accurate acerbity I came later on to recognise as well in character. No long time afterwards at breakfast with Forbes in Clare, the political back-chat (well above my head) evoked from Manny the startling phrase that Lloyd George, the Liberal Leader, was 'behaving like a prostituted vixen'. This earliest example of Manny's vivid style instantly appealed to me, but I reflected that it represented a break from the home background.

Impressions of dining in Hall at this time, December 1918, are blurred and overlaid by layers of later origin, but in one respect at least they are unique to this time for they include a visual recollection of an ultra-dignified white-bearded butler presiding over (or at least dominating) the High Table. This was the almost legendary Phipps who had been butler to the former, recently deceased Master, Dr Atkinson. As I later found, Phipps was the centre of many college legends based upon his unchallenged authority. One such story concerns the great Professor Ridgeway, alike great classical scholar and authority on the geological history of the horse, whose failing vision was so untrustworthy that it was said that although he was observed to be wearing a black tie before struggling with the ox-tail soup, it was absent when he allowed Phipps to take his plate. On this occasion, also as guest in Clare, he was presented with a small woodcock to dissect and incorporate. Seeing a flurry of ineffective struggle, Phipps' compassion moved him to lean forward over the Professor's shoulder, removing the dangerous dish with a confiding remark, 'it isn't worth it, sir; it isn't worth it.'

So little trace remained of Phipps after the war that I was delighted, some years later, calling with a botanical class for tea in a pub in Comberton, to find that this was run by members of the family and that Phipps' noble figure was well represented in the photographs decorating the parlour.

The award of the college scholarship in December and

supplementation by a County Council scholarship meant that I had nine months to wait before taking up residence in Cambridge, which I was assured might at that time be managed on a minimum of about £180 a year. I used my pre-university months to prepare for the London University Intermediate examination for the B.Sc., as insurance against a possible future need to sit for a London degree. For this purpose I required some knowledge of mineralogy and I was able to meet the need for the mineralogical microscope and prepared rock-slices by bicycling on Saturday mornings to the University Department of Geology in Nottingham, where that kindest and wisest of teachers, Professor H. H. Swinnerton, not only provided these necessities but produced and vetted for me exercises in the interpretation of geological maps and threw in many morsels of geological instruction that I have remembered ever since. He came to our help many years later when my wife and I sought to bring pollen-analytic methods to clarify the dating of the peat-beds on the Lincolnshire coast, long the subject of Swinnerton's careful recording.

III
FRESHMAN

So GREAT WERE THE CHANGES that accompanied my
translation from school to university in the autumn of 1919 that
the pallid phrase 'coming-up' is useless to describe them: the
experience had more in common with falling over a cliff, nor,
in retrospect does the experience seem less startling. It was, to
begin with, my first experience of living away from home, and
one entered a society where one made contacts with returned
servicemen hardened by extreme experience of danger and
hardship and where a majority of fellow students had been at
preparatory and public school. This latter imbalance of
schooling scarcely held, however, in the laboratories, for the
colleges were by now accustomed to taking many if not most
of their scientists from the country's grammar and secondary
schools, usually by way of scholarship awards. It was on these
schools that the country had almost exclusively depended for
its requirements in the technological parts of the services –
navigation, wireless and artillery ranging and so forth: the
important adaptation of the public schools took place later as
the country accepted the inevitable expansion of science into
every area of our existence, cultural or economic.

As undergraduate, now part of the population scrupulously
referred to as the 'men', I found myself having to take
responsibility for my own actions and decisions, whether to
work or to play, to attend more lectures or more games or more
politics or cinema or debates or theatre. The headiness of this
new freedom has been expressed acutely and accurately by
generations of university graduates looking back on this stage
of their own lives. For me the indecisions were ironed out to
a considerable extent by close financial constraint that meant
not only strict present limits on spending but a realisation that

my future depended on scholastic success so that classes and reading were not to be trifled with – not that this was so much a burden as a very welcome opportunity to learn and expand.

The changes in my own life-style I soon realised were coincident with a vast alteration in the customs and character of the college itself. So extensive had been the slaughter of the war and so horrifying the stresses of long sustained trench warfare with its high saturation of artillery fire, that the returned service men who now thronged the college screens before going in to dinner in Hall were unlike any generation before or since. Their eyes were haunted, but they all displayed a kindness to one another and a gentleness to the schoolboy freshmen that were all-embracing: it was enough that you and they were still living for them to offer a friendship embracing everything they were possessed of; to be alive and alongside other friendly humans was all Elysium. They never spoke of their own experiences to those too young to have shared them but concentrated on rebuilding a structure of college society, and some few of them had indeed returned to college specifically to reconstruct boat club, athletics or other component as it used to be and as they remembered it. The Second World War had a totally different reaction upon the returning population, for in 1939–45 there was no more calling-up of subalterns at eighteen, straight from the school O.T.C. to face a life-expectation in the trenches of two or three weeks. Instead all university men had one year before enrolment, there was far more selective employment in the services, and long spells of inactivity. Instead of long periods overseas away from home, the airforces might alternate strenuous warfare with recovery the same night on English soil. Moreover as we were all aware, the civilian population closely shared the direct dangers of warfare as they could not do in the first war. The return of men from service was altogether more gradual than after the First World War, and they entered college societies that had been far less scarified and diminished.

Although college and university retained for the most part

their traditional structure, changes were at work here also, and a pre-war 'freshman's guide' would have been astray in many details. The custom of paying and returning visits, complete with engraved 'visiting cards' was almost extinct at undergraduate level, and the convention that only Egyptian or Turkish cigarettes were acceptable had been submerged in a great wave of cigarette smoking in which ninety-nine per cent of the population engaged and in which only the Virginian 'fag' was ever used. It was still possible to buy hand-made oriental cigarettes, the rice paper printed with one's college arms, and a parcel as small as a box of a hundred would be delivered by errand boy at one's rooms. In general, however, the ban against carrying one's own shopping was now inoperative, though the big grocery stores like Matthews, Brimley Wibley, Hallack & Bond, and Flack & Judge, with their enchantingly odorous cavernous ranges of counters, would send composite orders booked by a student or, on his behalf, by his bedmaker. A particularly striking reminder of changes in another direction was given me when, in my first May term, I commented to Miss Ranson, my ageing landlady, upon the sudden prevalence of pretty women and lovely dresses in the town. 'Ah', she said, 'but you should have seen the place before the Fellows were allowed to marry: we had some fine ladies about then!'. The time was within her easy recollection when college societies were entirely of unmarried dons, save for the Master who, in a separate establishment, constituted with his family a distinct and utterly superior layer of university society limited to 'Heads of Houses'. The University Act requiring all dons to be unmarried had been repealed in 1882 but the college bodies were very slow to change from their original organisation as work places and homes for unmarried male scholars and to accept the fact that many of their members were married men with wives and children who command some of the time formerly given to collegiate common-room life.

When college life was resumed after the First World War, Clare was indeed a small college restricted by its endowments to about a dozen fellows, with an undergraduate population of roundabout 125 and with a single court which, although beautiful beyond all others in Cambridge, offered but scanty accommodation. Aside from lecture rooms, bursary, kitchen, rooms for resident dons, hall and chapel, there were available in the whole court only some thirty-five sets for undergraduates, many of these doubled. It followed that everyone spent at least one of this three student years in lodgings: only the needs of club secretaries, boat-captains and such others as needed to be near the notice-boards and porters' lodge, secured a longer foothold. The many lodgings were comfortable and close at hand, the rooms having the strong impress of black horsehair, polished mahogany, mantels with tasselated chenille hangings, a presiding black marble clock, window tables carrying an aspidistra (*ad astra*), and, in concession to the recent taste, a very elongated cane basket chair sprawling near the fire, at demonstrable risk of ignition. Occupants of the adjacent 'digs' might often be seen strolling in dressing gowns through the streets to enjoy a morning bath in college. A corresponding counter-flow, if it can be so called, could be seen at lunch or dinner time when some students in lodgings might order meals from college in their digs: they would be carried there in large deep-sided trays, insulated by heavy baize cloths, borne on the heads of skilful college porters.

Whether 'keeping' in digs or in college, one was expected to attend dinner in Hall on six nights a week where one's presence was pricked off by the buttery-clerk, Edgar, perforating a mounted attendance list: after the first day or two he had seldom to enquire a man's name, and failure to attend meant a summons to the tutor. No doubt regularity at Hall actively increased the coherence of the college as well as giving a guarantee of adequate nourishment for careless youth. The circumstances of dining were of course quite foreign to me. Food was ample and we were served at the vast oak tables by college servants, who, having dispensed the soup or fish, invariably enquired 'beef or mutton, sir?'. The meat was carved with the greatest expedition at the hot-plate by senior gyps who brought their own cherished cutlery for the purpose and gained no little kudos from their expertise. We used the college's heavy Victorian silver at table and for ordinary drinks from the buttery likewise had the use of Georgian or Victorian tankards or silver beakers given by past generations of Clare men. Of the alumni whose portraits sloped darkly down from the walls, I had prior knowledge of only one, Marquis Cornwallis, and of that able and distinguished diplomat and soldier all I then recollected was the embarrassing footnote to my history lessons that he 'surrendered at Yorktown, with 80,000 men'.

The hall itself was excellent late Jacobean, but its robust simplicity had been drenched and submerged in middle Victorian time by a plethora of applied carving and intricate variegated wall and ceiling decoration that left no panel untouched: it all stood greatly in need of cleaning and restoration, but opportunity for these arrived only with time and changes of college circumstances.

There was really no doubt that the true colour of college life was to be gained only by residence in the Old Court at whatever level one might achieve this. I was lucky enough to be assigned share in a double attic set at the head of E staircase, in the centre of the college's southern front, that range of building just completed when Cromwell's occupation of the town and commandeering of building material brought a stop for several years to the rebuilding of the court. It is thought that the Master consequentially had his Lodge on this staircase for it is still provided with a superb wooden staircase with massive newel posts, surmounted by fine finials supporting from each one to the next a long and neatly perforated oak plank, like fretwork performed by elephants. The staircase divided above into the steps leading to the two opposing sets of attic rooms, and between them was the window giving access to the leads of the roof. When unlocked, as it often was, it allowed one to contemplate at close quarters the magnificent square masonry chimneys on which so much of the aesthetic appeal of the building rests, the comfortable dormers, the fragile heavy and uncommon Collyweston slates, only too susceptible to any careless treading but of exceptionally beautiful texture. I found subsequently that Mansfield Forbes shared my delight in the beauty of the Clare roof scenery, and when be came to edit the *Book of Clare* he introduced others to these generally overlooked prospects, so that there are illustrations by many high-grade photographers, by J. F. Greenwood (wood-engraving) and by Sydney W. Carline (pencil drawings), all showing the Clare roof-scapes. A sight that has never failed to move me by its calm beauty is that of the two stone cherubs that, one on either side of the entrance gateway, spread protecting wings towards the centre of the court and in the moonlight of the small hours wear the aspect of guardian angels.

It is only fair to remark that the attic rooms had more down-to-earth qualities. The rooms were heated by open fires fed from a scuttle on the hearth that was replenished from a wooden bin on the staircase landing, to which coal was carried by the sack-load. We bathed after games in a tin hip-bath before the fire in a canful of hot water carried up by the gyp from the kitchens across the court. Adequate enough for this and for toasting muffins, the heat of the living room fire scarcely penetrated to my bedroom beyond the intervening gyp-room and in the harder winters the water in the hand-basin by my bed sometimes by morning carried ice over half-an-inch thick. In a mild season one would hear the sound of a rushing cataract of water, behind the wall alongside my bed: when curiosity impelled me to remove the covering panel, I found that a deep lead-linen wooden trough extended right through the thickness of the college, and in heavy rain it constituted a gutter draining all the roofing facing King's and carrying the water to down-pipes on the inside of the Clare courtyard. Whether we needed the water, or King's refused to take it, I never discovered, but I learned that the open gutter was liable to be a hazard when leaves choked its intake and locally flooded the roof-flats.

Roof-scape of the south range of the Old Court. According to Mansfield Forbes, King's Chapel resembles an elephant waiting to enter its pen

Oriel and pedimented gable of the east centre range of the Old Court of
Clare

Seventeenth-century porch that formerly stood over the rear-entrance to the buttery (H staircase)

25

The Clare ghost. The legendary perambulation of the medical skeleton collecting his bones from various parts of the Old Court, as shown in Paulopostprandials by Owen Seaman

The communicating gyp room between the double living-room and my bedroom was haunted by mice so that food needed to be stored in tins. I managed to control their access to some extent by stacking bundles of firelighters over the mouseholes at floor level: unfortunately the naphthalene, whose crystals spattered the bundles of sticks, had a strong affinity for butter, whose virginity was readily compromised if it was left exposed.

The old-world limitations of life in E8 were also recognisable elsewhere in the old Court, quite unmistakably in its sewage disposal that was centred upon a short range of earth-closets situated right by the river's brim, so far in fact that a friend of mine kept his bicycle after dark at the foot of H staircase to diminish the fatigue of the journey.

From the river one could see the blocked-up, but quite recognisable, archways in the brickwork of the walls fronting the Cam: these were not *oubliettes* from the Master's Lodge, useful as these no doubt could have been, but sewers now no longer permitted to discharge directly into the river. This row of privies made use of a simple mechanical device to dispense a shot of suitably disinfected earth into the waiting containers. This open air establishment, and early morning meeting-place, of course, was generally known as 'Lady Clare' (privily known,

'Bull-dogs'. Impression of the Proctor's constables pursuing an
undergraduate

one might well say), a custom that allowed much pleasant gross humour at the expense of the ignorant. When I had told my own G.P. in the Midlands that I was coming to reside in Cambridge he had told me that he himself was a native of the northern Fenland and that malaria was still endemic in those parts. Sure enough the river precincts of the Lady Clare swarmed with the malaria vector, the spotted-winged mosquito (*Anopheles maculipennis*) taking full advantage of feeding opportunities. One unfortunate man of my year who had never been outside England in his life, duly went down with the disease, alongside the occasional ex-service men suffering recurrences after an initial infection acquired overseas.

IV
THE EARLY 1920s

THE WAR had made extremely severe demands upon the small
fellowship of Clare, and the early 1920s were a time of much
readjustment. Chapel offices had been sustained by a self-
effacing and loyal chaplain who met the handicap of his
teutonic name 'Hof', by becoming Vesey-Hope. The office of
Dean was filled after the war by the Revd P. C. T. Crick of
whom primary recollection is of a muscular heartiness backed
up by sterling competence as a hockey-player: it seemed
appropriate that in 1920 he took off to become Bishop of
Rockhampton where he patrolled his extensive Queensland
diocese in pioneer fashion from the air. His place was taken by
W. Telfer, a man of the greatest courage and modesty who later
became Master of Selwyn College. It was a great pleasure in
later years to act with him as colleague, sharing college duties
and relaxations: more of this later. As my rooms on E8 were
vertically over the Dean's, he must have suffered considerably
when I enjoyed a phase of learning fencing and I remember
Telfer's modest comment that the shuffling was just tolerable
but the thump, at quite unpredictable intervals, would break
anyone's nerve. We shamefacedly desisted from further sword
play!

When I came up in 1919 the Senior Tutor was 'Jackie'
Wardale, a white-haired classics don and third of a devoted
sequence of Clare fellows bearing the family name. He sat me,
I remember, at his table and then found the correspondence
relating to me by fishing for it in the shoals lying in the large
wicker basket underneath it. In 1920, however, the tutorship
was taken over by a young physicist, Henry Thirkill, newly
returned from overseas service in South-east Africa, now in the
college interest relinquishing, for the time-being at least,

something of his research and teaching in the Cavendish laboratory. He was later to become full-time Senior Tutor, widely regarded as 'the best tutor in either University', and held in the greatest affection and respect by many generations of Clare men.

As undergraduate I naturally saw little of the other fellows excepting for Mansfield Forbes who kept up the kindly interest derived from my school background and his friendship with F. L. Attenborough. From time to time I was asked to one of Manny's fabulous Sunday morning breakfasts, with a most carefully chosen selection of hearties, aesthetes and passing visitors. I can still visualise the favourite dish from the kitchens, hot entrée dishes of 'Eggs à l'Aurore'. Manny's charm rapidly involved everyone in active conversation until about eleven o'clock when he took off the athletes for a walk in the countryside from which they returned somewhat before dusk, most of the party dog-tired but Manny's slight figure, hardened by long days on Scottish mountains, still fresh as a harebell. It must have been Manny who had some part in securing my election to the Clare 'Dilettanti', a club where a judicious mixture of men of aesthetic or generally cultural interests met for entertainment and discussion. I recall that at one of their meetings Hubert D. Henderson, fellow, recently economic adviser to Lloyd George and soon to become editor of the *Nation and Athenaeum*, described to us the process and events that in the recent history of Britain had brought us to the verge of war: he concluded by putting the case for the newly proposed League of Nations. On another occasion, Ffrangcon Roberts, medical fellow of the college, outlined for us the principles of psycho-analysis, a subject unfamiliar but attracting attention as part of the widespread occurrence of psychic disorders in the extreme stresses of trench warfare. We were not then aware of the involvement of the Cambridge psychologist W. H. R. Rivers in the later publicised breakdown of Siegfried Sassoon, one of the greatest of Clare's authors, whose *Memoirs of an Infantry Officer* was a deserved classic of the First World War.

Silhouettes. The Dean, W. Telfer (later Master of Selwyn); the Master
W. L. Mollison; H. Thirkill, subsequently Master and Vice-Chancellor

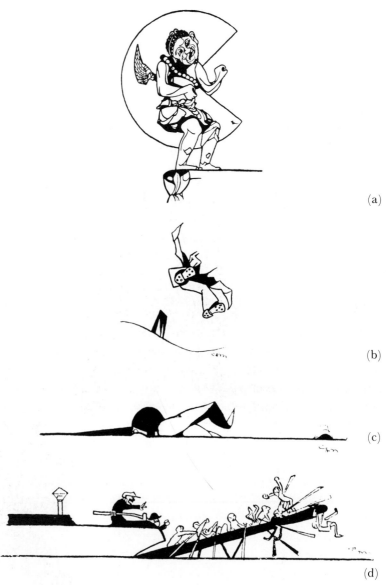

Head and Tail pieces, for various college societies' accounts: (a) the Dilettanti, (b) cricket, (c) swimming, (d) rowing

The freshman taking up residence in college, especially if he had no circle of school friends already with experience of the system, was singularly indebted to the helpfulness of the gyp or bedmaker responsible for the eight or so sets upon his staircase. As I remember him in the person of my own gyp, Edward Hall, he was, as my small sister used to misquote, 'a very pleasant help in time of trouble'. He could at short notice provide the loan of a kettle or even, in emergency, a gown, he reminded one of the time of tutorial appointments and was a never-failing source of information on local geography and on both college and university customs. At this time poorly paid, some of the servants moved to jobs in seaside hotels during the Long Vacation and practically all waited at our meals in Hall. Tips from the men on the staircase were a significant source of income that had careful consideration by all the resident population.

Hall was a florid-faced, fat and jocular man who had his great moment when called as witness at the 'Moot' in the College Hall, where, when asked his name, he replied with that of one of the best-known of King's Counsel, namely Sir Edward Marshall Hall, thereby creating suitable confusion. One spring afternoon Hall chose to stay on the staircase when the men had gone out to football, and giving way to prankish impulse he built up from cardboard rolls pushed inside items of spare clothing, the effigy of a huddled old oriental gentleman sitting by the fire wrapped in overcoat and scarf. His wrinkled brown face, when the occupant returned from his rugger game, proved to be a coconut, partly husked, carved and painted like a face. It had been borrowed from elsewhere on the staircase and Hall took care to be at hand to view the reception of his creation.

More sober-sided, although not unhumorous, was Maltby on the Tutor's staircase, so conscientious that he was commonly waiting with his bicycle at the College gate when it opened at six a.m. He had strongly Christian principles and was so deeply concerned with the success of the Sunday-school classes he ran that he might on occasions try to recruit as teacher for them any of his 'men' whom he sufficiently approved of: I was not aware of any acceptances.

Each day breakfast would be laid for us in the sitting-room and a significant part of it was the fresh milk, butter and newly baked loaf that each man received as 'commons'. Likewise a cold lunch was laid to which a small Winton-Smith pork pie or a small tin of corned-beef made the major contribution: rationing was still in force and kitchen and buttery regularly took the coupons they needed. It was established custom that bedmakers took home at the end of the day the left-over perishable foods and they had access to what now would be regarded as a cherished culinary by-product, large basins of beef-dripping from the kitchens. Dripping from this source was regularly on sale in shops in the town centre.

None of the college servants was more readily recognisable than Parsons, the kitchen-manager, whose elongated cadaverous figure brooded over mealtimes and spread the air of sadness like the character in the 'Arcadians' who regularly intoned 'I've got a motto... "always merry and bright"'. Parsons was invariably known as 'Sandow', an ironic reference to the familiar advertisements of the muscular and confident strong man, Eugène Sandow. When approached to provide a special meal for some celebration, he assumed an air of deep depression and announced that it was 'very difficult to get anything now', but then he would tentatively offer a fresh salmon, and enquire if a pheasant followed by *crème brulée* would perhaps make do: in short, he could, and did, provide an excellent repast from the cloud of foreboding.

The best of the Sandow stories relates to the early period when G. H. A. Wilson, then bursar, was living in college and taking breakfast from the kitchens. After suffering the dreadfulness of the porridge for as long as he might, the bursar summoned Parsons and confronted him with the dish. 'Look, Parsons', he said, 'it's lumpy, and smoky and it's burnt...here take it, and taste it.' Sandow shrank back in horror. 'Wot, not me, sir, I never touch it: food for 'ogs I call it!' It was much to the bursar's credit that he himself perpetuated the story of this knock-out blow, worthy of the strong-man prototype.

It was natural that from the time I began work for the Tripos I should be introduced to the system of 'supervision', that arrangement whereby in Oxford and Cambridge the colleges made themselves responsible for their students' progress in a manner totally independent of university authority. For my own part I found the small weekly interviews, with associated writing, preparation and half-professorial gossip to be of the utmost value, especially in my two chief subjects, botany and geology. For the former subject I came under F. T. Brooks of Emmanuel, a staunch Somerset man, Lecturer in Botany and later to become professor. He was a most experienced mycologist returned to Cambridge after some war-time work on crop-diseases in the Tropics. His classes naturally tended to have a strong fungal flavour and I inclined much to mycology, but he was also entirely sympathetic to ecology and it suited me that I was invited to join all his advanced field excursions.

In geology I had the advantage of tuition from E. W. Ravenshear who had come up to Clare as a scholar in 1912. I learned a great deal from his approach, especially an introduction to Jukes-Browne's highly stimulating text-book *The Building of the British Isles*. My gains were bought, however, at a considerable price, for our classes, on Monday evenings, were on an upper floor of lodgings in Great St Mary's Chambers, slap opposite the belfry of the University Church and during bell-ringing practice. It was next door to intolerable and gave me great sympathy for another Clare undergraduate, who greeted the racket of the constant chiming of the town with moans of 'Damn those bells, those bloody, bloody bells', and finally shifted his lodgings to the distant Rock Estate, halfway to the Gog-Magogs. I cherish from this time my recollection of a more informal supervision given purely out of affection for his subject, by Dr T. G. Bonney of St John's College. He was a venerable, bearded and bent figure who leaned over my shoulder as I looked at the lava specimens in the 'Students'

Series' at the Sidgwick Museum, told me that such and such were the qualities of this Icelandic lava and he drew pictures of the fissures as he had seen them on Mt Hekla. Bonney's venerability and eminence were suitably acknowledged by the Tripos class when the lecturer said, in a throw-away tone that 'the best guide to the geology of the Cambridge region remains that of Dr Bonney, published in 1875'.

I discovered quite early that a scientist who had three practical laboratory subjects was obliged to give up at least three afternoons a week to one of them (the other two having alternate morning times) and this commitment, along with week-end field excursions, effectively excluded college team games. However, lack of interests has never been a problem in the undergraduate environment and in these particular years two activities caught up the fullest attention of the place. The most notable of these was the jape so superbly organised by returned service men of Caius College. They had been put out by the offer to their college of a war trophy of inferior grade to the field-piece allocated to Jesus College, and attempts having failed to switch the respective destinations along the route via Cambridge Railway Station, they were faced by the fact of the Jesus gun bolted to a concrete base. Nevertheless, when the Caius front gate opened next morning and the forewarned reporters swarmed in, the Jesus gun had miraculously preceded them. The university duly relished the detailed story of how the key to the long-unopened Gate of Honour had been secured and replicated, how scouts thus escaped from college had entered Jesus grounds and lying beneath the gun had sawn off the securing bolts, whilst colleagues silently cut out a section of the boundary fencing. At this stage, police attention suitably distracted elsewhere, a further team with soft shoes and blackened faces, muffled the wheel rims and metal traces, and finally hauled the piece silently away to enter Caius from the King's Parade, there to be fastened behind the re-closed gate whose false key reached the ooze beneath the Cam. A tiny toy gun was left on the Jesus gun emplacement, and to everyone's satisfaction, no one had heard anything.

Likewise within the years just after the War we were involved in a sequence of communal jokes for which the term 'rag' is altogether too boisterous. They were above all good-natured, witty and quite free from any kind of hooliganism. If I remember properly, the first was the 'Pavement Club' for which the undergraduate newspaper summoned everyone to attend on Saturday mid-morning on King's Parade, there to practise an hour or two of *dolce far niente*. Undergraduates came in shoals on what proved to be a fine day, and sat down with cushions, newspapers, dominoes, coffee, and similar aids to civilised living, occupying alike pavements and roadways in a friendly open-air club that dispersed momentarily when asked to do so by the infinitely out-numbered police, but directly moving back again. The members immensely relished their own gesture, so successful that it was never repeated although later on there was an open-air cookery competition held in the Market Place for small teams providing their own utensils and raw materials.

Later again there was the altogether more pretentious 'Opening of the tomb of Tutankhamun' at the climax of which 'angels' descending from the old cinema in the Market pointed out the tomb entrance, which, recognisable as the public lavatory, yielded up a heavily wrapped mummy. This was decorticated to reveal no less a figure than the wooden Scottish highlander, *Phineas*, the mascot of University College, London, borrowed from the doorway of Catesby's furniture store in the Tottenham Court Road for this occasion. I never gathered that D. A. Catesby, a scholar in Clare at the time, had the least bit to do with the event, any more for that matter than had Sir Leonard Woolley.

It is pleasurable to cast one's mind back and recall some incident or other that has had a degree of historical authenticity about it. Thus I took some trouble to attend an open lecture given by Gilbert K. Chesterton in the old Victoria Cinema. After the familiar jest recounting how his weight was too much for the floor-boards of the hansom, so that he arrived at the run, Chesterton engaged us upon the theme so dear to him, that the last few centuries of British history demonstrated that in casting off the mild and beneficent rule of the Roman Catholic church, we had placed upon ourselves, from Puritan times forward, ever harsher and more restrictive manacles. Comment after the lecture centred on the gaunt and formidable figure of G. G. Coulton, the schoolmaster research fellow of St John's exposing in a ruthless scholastic style a historic version of medieval ecclesiastical history notably less attractive than the lecturer's. The Chairman eventually terminated the deeply felt altercation by proposing that discussion should continue in the *Cambridge Review*. From this sustained debate arose the poem by Belloc, attaining more permanence than the lecture that had begun it. We all recall at least the opening lines, 'remote and ineffectual don, that dared attack my Chesterton...'; by no means so ineffectual, of course, although engaging his fire on targets not always popular, as one may see in his marvellous biography *Fourscore Years*, recipient of the national James Tait Black prize.

A historical link of very different quality came my way as an undergraduate, when through my mathematical room-mate I learned the story of the war-time activity of one of the earliest 'boffins', Gilbert West, Clare scholar of 1916. He and a fellow physicist found themselves in the second half of the War working in an isolated hut on the flat coast of Essex, engaged in developing the possibilities of the infant science of 'wireless' and in particular of the possibilities of directional radio reception. At this time the German High Seas fleet was confined to its harbour in Kiel whilst the British Battle Fleet stood guard waiting for its emergence into the North Sea. This frustration had lasted a considerable time when one night West picked up by his directive antennae a message broadcast clearly by German Naval Command, under the impression that no message could be intercepted beyond about one hundred miles range. What was more, it was an order to the German fleet to proceed at once to sea. It wonderfully well reflects the contemporary status of the 'boffin' that our young physicist at this juncture had no telephone and had to pedal off on his bike to rouse the local postmistress who spent two or three hours raising the appropriate section of the Admiralty. Nonetheless, informed they were, and back the information went to the waiting ships of the Battle Fleet. In this way were taken the opening steps of the Battle of Jutland, and so modest was Gilbert West about it all that it was not until his own son Richard came to me for supervision after the Second World War that the story at last reached the next generation.

V

TRIPOSES

WITH THE COURSES for the Natural Sciences Tripos in Botany, I began in 1919 the close association with the Cambridge Botany School that has been unbroken up to the present day: the trifling hiccough of retirement from the headship of the Department glossed over generously by an Emeritus Professorship and the kindnesses of my two successors.

Professor A. C. Seward, at this time Master of Downing College, gave the elementary lectures for the whole of the first year himself, in the form of a course comprehensible to complete beginners. It was primarily a survey of the various groups of the Plant Kingdom from the simplest of algae and fungi to the most advanced flowerless and flowering plants. Supplemented by laboratory examination and generous displays of living material grown in the Botanic Garden, this course had great intrinsic interest for all who were in any way drawn to study of the natural history of plants. Seward was a fine lecturer and the reputation of his courses continued to reach one at encounters with old Cambridge men many years afterwards. When I came to undertake my own first lectures I recall that I thought so highly of the Professor's technique that I made my way to listen beneath the floor of the lecture theatre to hear, not the *matter* of Seward's lectures, but the delivery and style he employed, his pace, emphasis, measured pause and change of pitch. He commanded full attention, and the audiences were large. This was a matter of no small importance, for at that time each departmental head ran his school on the fees he collected from students going to the lectures and practical classes provided by the staff: such fees depended very largely upon attendances at the first year courses, whose popularity in turn rested largely upon experienced tutorial recommendation. This system prevailed up to the change of university statutes in 1925 and its impact on the teaching staff was illustrated by the story of Henry Thirkill's own experience when he was himself demonstrator in the Cavendish Laboratory under the great J. J. Thomson. Henry recounts that on a snowy Christmas Eve he encountered his Professor on King's Parade, and after an enquiry whether he had yet been paid his term's salary, and a negative reply, J. J. said, 'never mind, just make a back under this street lamp', and proceeded to find his cheque book and write out and hand over a suitable order for payment.

Although botanical taxonomy had a long pre-Darwinian medical history, Seward's survey of the Plant Kingdom was naturally threaded together by evolutionary relationships, to some degree necessarily deduced from comparative study of life-histories and structure, but to a stimulating extent; since Seward was one of the most eminent of the world's palaeobotanists, the fossil plant record was brought in to bear upon the evolutionary argument. The appeal of the course as a whole was enhanced by Seward's pleasant habit of circulating in the practical classes, so that he soon had direct familiarity with each of his students: it was a trait illustrative alike of his friendly enthusiasm and of his tirelessness. There is, of course, great advantage in having a single lecturer for all three consecutive terms. A close intimacy can develop between lecturer and audience and an awareness of shared jokes and attitudes, whilst there is small danger of breaks or gaps between even distant areas of argument.

It will come as no surprise that Seward's sympathy with his class gave him exceptional audience control. Lectures began precisely at five past ten and of the class of 200 or so, few risked coming in later. One exceptional day, however, as the Professor came within a few minutes of the conclusion of his lecture, a lone student strolled in, and at leisure descended the long lateral flight of steps, looking for a vacant seat, which, found towards the middle of a front row, was taken with total nonchalance. Seward had politely paused and the class waited, silent and apprehensive of the fate about to overtake such outrageous presumption. In the pause Seward smiled in the kindest possible manner and remarked, 'It's awfully good of you to look in on us this morning.' The latecomer was buried in the paroxysms of laughter from the class. I learned afterwards that he went to apologise to the Professor, who entirely accepted his story that after working late, the victim had overslept, but full of virtue and secure in the belief that the lecture was just due to begin, had sauntered along taking the time to be a whole hour earlier than it was!

It might have been assumed that so full a course as Seward's, supplemented by at least six hours of laboratory work each week, together with preparation set by F. T. Brooks for his weekly supervision-classes, would have satiated my appetite, but not so. I discovered in the Botany School library a source of unexpected riches in the text books of ecology, especially the massive and diverse works of the American, F. E. Clements. I waded deeply into these and Tansley's *Types of British Vegetation*, with sundry special excursions into the pastures provided by the *Journal of Ecology* and its American counterpart, *Ecology*. It was not altogether surprising that a good deal else in the Tripos work was neglected, with consequences revealed to Tutorial gaze when the collegiate 'Mays' examination results appeared. A much more selective system of work followed in my second year.

I took this occasion also to teach myself to write. Having at the last moment discovered that a whole term's lecture notes, scribbled down hastily, were illegible and quite useless, I set about the exercise of inventing a new calligraphy in which each letter was chosen so as to be most simply, quickly, and economically written in cursive linkage with its neighbours. I chose a flexible finger-hold and practised the new style for a few weeks, and to my own surprise found I had indeed literally at hand a new, fast and legible style: it has served me ever since.

In the second year course for the botanical student in the Tripos, F. T. Brooks lectured upon the variation in life-cycles, and the elements of genetics and cytology, F. F. Blackman upon the physiology and biochemistry of the plant-cell, whilst A. G. Tansley in the short May term gave a brief introduction to some aspects of plant ecology associated with life form.

None of the three courses bore direct relation to the first year lectures, but they all represented aspects of botanical science at that time newly struggling to become established. No general text-book covered their scope and in a broad sense they were certainly part of the consequence of application of the physical sciences, with their qualitative and experimental methods and improved technology to the fields of biological research. The expansion was at this time so recent that no formal practical work accompanied any of these lecture courses.

In the absence of any indigenous botanist in Clare there was, from 1919 onwards, an arrangement with F. T. Brooks, himself an Emmanuel man, that he should supervise all Clare botanists reading for the Tripos. Accordingly for the next three years I came under his direction, writing weekly essays for his correction and comment and listening to his gloss upon lectures I was attending or issues raised in reading. As followed from the supervisor's chief interest, the discussions had a strongly myco-logical bent and I was enabled to attend the advanced field excursions he organised for the Part II Tripos people. From these I derived great pleasure and instruction, developing the habit (common with plant pathologists) of focussing attention less upon healthy plants of the countryside than upon the blotched, yellowed and rusted vegetable victims of plant diseases. These specimens we harvested with the care usually reserved for the unsullied perfect flowering plant, and in the laboratory later on the host and disease were examined, drawn, recorded and identified, aided greatly by Saccardo's *Index*. At this time the Part II Tripos course was nominally of two years duration and Brooks, making use of a convenient natural division of the Fungi, lectured in one year upon one half, and in the alternate year upon the other half of it. Already determined to read Part II Botany, I attended one of these

F. F. Blackman F.R.S., St John's College, doyen of plant physiologists

courses in my second year of Part I studies, so simplifying the compression of the Part II course into a single third year, a procedure now become general, although arduous.

It is not surprising that such a course of study left me deeply interested in mycology and a career as plant pathologist looked both promising and possible, not least because one proved able to advise farmers and gardeners on identification and treatment of the commoner plant diseases of their crops. Brooks had every right to think that I might indeed join the very flourishing research school he directed, but I never concealed from him my overriding concern with the emergent subject of ecology, nor did he ever seek to deflect me from moving into that area of botany.

From the days of my special concern with mycology I recall with relish an encounter in a small country town near Newark with a fine display of the 'silver-leaf' disease of fruit trees. My supervisor was an authority upon its habit and treatment and it had been made subject of a national notification order intended to secure total eradication of diseased trees and of every stump and branch bearing the crustose purple brackets that spread its innumerable spores. The local police-station displayed the large coloured notice of the disease on the brick wall facing across the street advising all and sundry of the penalties of non-notification. Over the wall alongside in the sunshine there drooped a fine display of the generously silvered branches of a large diseased plum-tree. It was quite unrecognised by police or passers-by and I did not enlighten them. In time the large growers took heed and set up a system of effective orchard hygiene: certainly the disease is no longer so prevalent as formerly.

It may have struck the reader how little time in either the first- or second-year courses was devoted to the study of the flowering-plant as it grows naturally, and the cause for this, it has been suggested, lies in the late-mediaeval origins of the universities. The student calendar appears directly to have been adjusted to the agricultural cycle, freedom to attend college only arising when crops had been gathered in the autumn, and persisting until the farms claimed student labour once more for cultivation and planting in late spring. Anyone responsible for botanical teaching in Britain will realise that the first spring growth in woodlands and waysides is hardly to be glimpsed before the year's final examinations are upon one in May, and when the men arrive for their first term the leaves are turning colour and most summer flowers are gone. This chronological disposition, so awkward for botany, has long been met in English universities by a special system of ancillary field-excursions. Thus it is a well-established custom that in Cambridge during the week-ends or lighter evenings of the May term members of the staff concerned with field-studies should 'lay on' expeditions into the countryside to be attended voluntarily. Of at least equal importance is the arrangement of excursions lasting two or three weeks in the Easter and Summer vacations at localities of special botanical interest, not necessarily confined to the British Isles. Such parties make great demands on the energy and time of a few devoted members of the staff, who find themselves well repaid, however, by the enthusiastic response, often maintained in later years, from the active participants.

It will be readily perceived that the provision by the colleges of a 'Long Vacation' term of residence, also offers to botanists an ideal opportunity, not available in the three official university terms, to arrange both field excursions and field experimentation at the season of year when plant-growth is fully active and long days allow sustained observation. Very often such visits to special localities allow repetition of observations from year to year, a process especially helpful to ecological study in habitats such as woodland, fen or salt-marsh.

I moved from Part I Tripos work to that for Part II during the Summer vacation of 1921, and was at once aware of what could be called a sharp shift of gear. One was now concerned with a single subject only, and competition for laboratory and lecture room accommodation kept the class size down to only a dozen or thereabouts. Most significant, however, was the immediate alteration in the mental approach required. No longer was the text-book the prime source of information: we were directly referred to the original publications within the scientific journals and were expected to keep abreast of all recent developments of research in the subject as they appeared in the leading botanical journals of Britain, of France, Germany, Japan and the U.S. at least, as well as in *Nature* and similar periodicals of wide range. The course in botany had originally been designed to occupy two years but had now been compressed into one, and not surprisingly the classes and final examinations allowed a considerable degree of specialisation on one or a few of the major sections; taxonomy, plant physiology and biochemistry, mycology, palaeobotany, morphology and ecology. Substantial laboratory classes accompanied all the lecture course options and we were not excused a general paper embracing the whole field of botany. It was an extremely strenuous course that could not be recommended for cissies.

The combination of specialisation in the courses and direct reference to the areas of active research placed the scope and status immediately within the direction of the senior staff of the department, many of whom already enjoyed very high reputation internationally. Not least of these was Professor Seward himself, since 1906 administrative head of the department, a man of enormous strength and energy, formerly Tutor of Emmanuel College, appointed Master of Downing in 1915, President of the Geological Society of London in 1922 and Vice-Chancellor of the University in 1924. Brought originally into palaeobotany through the advice of McKenny Hughes of Clare, he became a world authority in that subject, less as a field geologist and collector than as collator and author of a classic series of standard reference works and effective general exposition such as *Plant Life Through the Ages*.

In the year when I completed Part II, Seward had, however, taken part (with R. E. Holttum, later to be Director of the Botanic Garden, Singapore) in an expedition to West Greenland. The Eocene plant fossils seen there as well preserved casts were not adequate for exact naming of the trees that they represented, but Seward recognised that on general ecological and anatomical grounds, such large and delicate leaves were totally unsuitable to growth in the latitudes where the fossils now occurred. Despite much opposition (if not derision), Seward suggested that these facts bore out the hypothesis of 'continental drift' then being strongly put forward by the geographer Wegener. There is no doubt that Seward's steady support for this view influenced many palaeontologists and biogeographers despite the opposition of geophysicists who tended to reject the facts of former plant and animal distribution because they saw no acceptable physical explanation of the massive earth displacements that were called for. The revolution in scientific attitude to one of approval for continental drift took many years to realise and I cherish the recollection of a scientific meeting in 1956 in Dunedin, when for the first time I saw physical and biogeographical conclusions firmly coincide. Under the aegis of E. C. Bullard, research into the palaeomagnetism of rock had been actively developed in the Cambridge Sub-department of Geophysics, whence Professor S. K. Runcorn had carried the successful techniques to Australia. Now some years of geophysical research in the Australasian region had securely established the main features of the dated shifts from one geological era to another, and presently he reported how they had confirmed the successive positions of the great crustal land-masses of South Africa, Antarctica, Australia and New Zealand. To this same meeting of the Australian and New Zealand Association for the Advancement of Science, came Dr R. D'O. Good who had been in my Cambridge Part II Tripos class thirty-four years earlier but who had since become one of the world's greatest plant geographers. Arriving in Dunedin after a protracted study tour across Indonesia and the Pacific, he was able to disclose how the present range of genera and families of plants still growing over this territory had enabled him to formulate an explanatory pattern of continental separation and conjunction that in all major respects was similar to that adduced by Runcorn. I thought of the satisfaction it would have given Seward to have witnessed this conjunction of his favourite sciences. It was still to be some years before the mechanism of 'Plate tectonics' allowed general acceptance of 'continental drift', but few now feel they lack at least the illusion of comprehending its mechanism.

In face of the immensely complicated nature of the living protoplasm now accepted as the essential primary substance of plant and animal cells, it was natural that, at the end of the last century, plant and animal physiologists should have been driven back to think in terms of a *vital life-force* and to think of processes as the *reaction* of the *irritable* protoplasm in response to outside *stimulus*. If explanation this was, it did not greatly promote further comprehension. It was therefore of particular relevance that we in Cambridge had the advantage of being taught by Mr F. F. Blackman of St John's, who, more than any other, had sought to establish the doctrine that all biological phenomena, like those of non-living systems, were to be interpreted *au fond* in terms of the laws of physics and chemistry. He had indeed devoted his Presidential Address to the Botanical Section of the 1908 meeting of the British Association explicitly to this theme. He incidentally then employed the startling remark that, considered from the recommended viewpoint, there was little difference between peeling a potato and flaying a saint. No doubt this had special appeal at a meeting in Ireland.

Already by the 1920s the battle had been effectively won, in considerable part through the exact thought and precise experimentation of Blackman's own research. Now his Part II

Tripos lectures were models of similar exactitude, warmly appreciated and attended not only by Tripos students but by research students and visitors from other biological departments, attracted in part by the fact that data discussed were from Blackman's own records unpublished elsewhere, and in part by their unmatched style of presentation.

I need not now point to the remarkable part played by Blackman as college and departmental administrator, as research supervisor or member of the Fitzwilliam Museum Syndicate, but one cannot omit his biographer's comment that 'He had the great teacher's quality of inspiring reverence.'

Another scientist of comparable rank on the staff at this time was Blackman's close friend over many years, Mr A. G. Tansley (later Sir Arthur Tansley) of Trinity College. In the congested space of the department he made do with a segment of the elementary laboratory cut off by matchboarding and chicken-wire, for he was no experimentalist and needed only space for the traffic in manuscripts of the two botanical journals that he edited, and for his own writing. He was a superb editor and the exceptional lucidity and fluency with which he wrote characterised also his Tripos lectures. Tansley's leadership of ecological thought was so extensive and reached both scientific and general public so effectively that more than anyone in this country he was accepted fully in this role.

Of the Botany School senior staff best known to me was F. T. Brooks, my College supervisor since 1919, who, having entered Emmanuel College in 1902, had read Botany and become most deeply attached to the brilliant teaching of Professor Marshall Ward, whose untimely death in 1906 left Brooks an almost open mandate to carry on the teaching of plant pathology in Cambridge along the lines already indicated by one he already appeared to venerate: certainly thus aided or no, Brooks now ceaselessly built up the Cambridge school into a world-renowned centre of research and of training in mycology and plant pathology.

In 1927 my career was decisively altered by the appointment of S. M. Wadham (later to become Sir Samuel Wadham, to the Chair of Agriculture in Melbourne, Australia. The post of Senior Demonstrator, now vacated by him was one of considerable standing, since it carried responsibility for adminstrating the large Elementary Laboratory along with the practical course for Part I of the Tripos and for first-year medical training for which it provided the necessary teaching and materials. I gladly accepted the offer to succeed to this post that I held with sustained interest and satisfaction until 1934. It was not until I had taken up the new post, with its necessarily close contacts with the head of the Botany School, Professor Seward, that Sam Wadham made me privy to the knowledge shared by a group of the senior staff as to the mental stability of their colleague, F. T. Brooks. They had early recognised that Brooks bore a serious antagonism to Seward, possibly stemming from the feeling that Seward had never been the equal of Marshall-Ward, the man he had succeeded in 1906. I was to discover that this antagonism was to persist intensely right up to the time of Brooks' death in 1952. Already however, during the First World War it had expressed itself dramatically when Brooks denounced Seward to the police as a German spy. Following this incident, a few of the older staff sought the advice of a leading London alienist by providing what evidence they had come to possess. On the strength of this they had been told that the behaviour pattern exhibited a strong paranoid tendency, extending even to the possibility of physical attack upon Seward. Wadham naturally felt uneasy at leaving Britain without advising me of the situation and the evident inadvisability of leaving Seward and Brooks alone together could this be avoided. Here indeed was a pretty kettle of fish for the new demonstrator, made no easier by the apparent unawareness of Seward as to how serious matters might be. At twenty-six I found the prospect alarming: I never had reason to doubt the accuracy of the diagnosis although happily no extreme crisis arose. In time Brooks extended his antagonism to everyone whom he regarded as favoured by his arch-enemy along with H. Gilbert-Carter, Director of the Botanic Garden.

As one came to realise later, Brooks' condition was very likely associated with his consuming devotion to his wife, a former research colleague, who had become severely deranged so as to require commitment to a mental hospital. As Brooks developed increasing signs of paranoia it seemed more than likely that the intensity of feeling between husband and wife had generated the condition then spoken of as *folie à deux*. Oddly enough I had not long been in my new post, when, meeting Seward at the pre-lecture consultation, he had handed me a coloured picture-postcard addressed to himself by the overcrowded display upon it of every title and form of address to which he could lay claim. The substance of the message was not important but Seward said that he supposed it to have come from one of Brooks' lunatic pals and that he would hand it on for comment. I begged the Professor to think again and heard no more of the episode, quite certainly a strayed missive from Mrs Brooks, such as this, could have created a real conflagration. When Seward retired from his headship of the department in 1936 he was succeeded by Brooks so that between that date and 1948 I had many years experience of this unpredictable and choleric personality.

It needs to be stressed that Brooks brought to the Chair of Botany many attributes of value, especially those that I emphasize in Chapter xvi, his industry, organisational ability and his unquestioned devotion to botany. Those of us who have followed Brooks in the headship of the Department are especially grateful for his foresight in leaving to the University a bequest which provides the Professor of Botany with funds from which he can meet the manifold minor claims provoked unexpectedly by teaching and research. The need had first impressed Brooks through the plight of research students from the Dominions engaged on the Cambridge three-year Ph.D. course with a grant sufficing only for two years. With care the 'Brooks Fund' has grown to a very useful means whereby the head of the Botany School can, at his own discretion, help along such problems as the sudden need for new apparatus, participation in field-excursion or scientific congress or prolongation of some research enquiry newly become urgent. Not a few research workers now eminent and successful, owe timely support to this source when some serious and critical need had to be met.

Our practical classes in Part I of the Tripos in 1919–21 were aimed to complement the Professor's lectures upon the whole plant kingdom by our own direct investigation of living and preserved material set before us on the laboratory benches and examined directly and by microscopy. To this end we learned some adroitness in cutting hand-held razor sections that were dehydrated, stained and mounted for examination and drawing. Essentially we were engaged on a general acquisition of information upon the anatomy and life history of plants: there was some slaughter of razor strops improperly used but human casualties were few. When we moved on to Part II of the Tripos we occupied a far smaller laboratory, intimate and serving the purposes of tea-room, lecture room and preparation counter all in one: we now were taught the art of serial sectioning by microtome and the room was dominated by a rank of copper ovens containing our tiny plant specimens simmering in molten wax. It did not represent much of an advance in technology, but it allowed us to look effectively into the mechanisms of meiosis (reduction division) then being newly described by V. H. Blackman of Imperial College. We used immature buds of the cultivated hyacinth and only later realised how the use of such hybrid material complicated our task. Brooks had a distracting habit of reiterating in his lectures many high-faluting catch-phrases to support his accounts of the virulence of plant-diseases. One best remembers 'spreading like wild-fire', 'in an epidemic manner' and 'one, as regards the other'.

Light-hearted students would keep tally of the recurrence of a favourite phrase so that large ticks or crosses freely littered the margins of our lecture-notes.

At a lower level of seniority in the staff were several who were also later to achieve international reputation. The palaeobotanist, H. Hamshaw Thomas, had at that time recently returned from active service with the Royal Flying Corps in the Middle East where he had played an important role in the development of aerial photography, an activity he applied successfully to the problems of vegetational survey, and subsequently in the Second World War, to aerial reconnaissance for Bomber Command. Also practising palaeobotany was John Walton, later to become Professor of Botany in Glasgow. Under Mr Blackman, G. E. Briggs (later to become head of the Cambridge Botany School himself) organised for our use a version of the ancient physiological experiments employed by Darwin and Acton, presenting it with typically astringent criticism. The Senior Demonstrator responsible for conduct of the Elementary Laboratory I have already mentioned as S. M. Wadham of Christ's. Lastly I might fairly add that when I was just launching into the full tide of botanical tuition, there returned to Cambridge Humphrey Gilbert-Carter, to take post as the first Director of the University Botanic Garden and to begin a career of remarkable influence on the future of taxonomic botany in Cambridge and over much wider fields.

VI

EMBARKING ON RESEARCH

WHEN in 1922 I turned from reading for the Tripos to commencing research, I found the mental break an extremely significant one. No doubt it remains so for all students, placed as they are so that the whole of their future may now be determined by choice of aim and adviser. It is a change just as fundamental as the earlier step from schoolboy to undergraduate, a sudden acceleration of growing-up and a new access to adult independence.

Provision for research was at this time far more meagre than now, and although under Seward the botanical department was a flourishing one, not more than a single research studentship became newly available each year. This was provided in alternate years by the Department of Scientific and Industrial Research and by the university 'Frank Smart' studentship. With a Part II Tripos class of ten to fifteen, this meant in effect that not only was a first class in the examination a necessity if one were to get an award, but also that one's results and prospects should appeal to the staff. In my own year preference rested with a plant physiologist friend, but my prospects were saved by the college introducing and awarding to me its earliest research studentship, alongside my appoinment as Junior Demonstrator on the Botany School staff. Very few colleges at this time gave research studentships, or, for that matter, had fellowships specifically for research, so that I was particularly indebted to Clare.

The choice of my prospective field of research offered some difficulty. On the one hand I was deeply attracted to ecology and especially to the meeting-ground of that subject with plant physiology, and on the other I recognised in Mr Blackman a scientist of world authority, training by whom would offer experience of quantitative and experimental methods less available if one began ecological research directly, even under Mr Tansley, eminent as he also was. The difficulty of choice was reflected in the anxiety of the dreams I had, one of which, as I vividly remember, involved a theatre stage where one of the leading actors was an impressive negro. At this period I had been much interested in Freudian dream-analysis and so spent considerable time trying to understand my dream: its main significance emerged as I saw that the dream symbolism had the negro for Blackman, and thereafter it became evident that my worry was over the dilemma of choice. In the event I was accepted by Mr Blackman and shortly afterwards I learned that my anxieties of choice had been pointless, since Tansley had in any event arranged to go to work with Freud in Vienna and could not have undertaken to supervise me.

Research in the Botany School was an intensely critical discipline, and nowhere more so than among the plant physiologists. One became personally responsible for one's results and arguments, irrespective of what current and popular views might be. One took an exhaustive survey of all that had been written and was thought in one's own field and proceeded thence in the hope of adducing data and conclusions that no reasonable and informed scientist could reject: it was one's aim to add one more component, small as it might be, to the corpus of accepted scientific knowledge.

Mr Blackman had the aptitude, invaluable in a supervisor, of exactly evaluating the needs of his various students for support and advice: some he interviewed regularly each day, checking the previous twenty-four hours' results and outlining the consequent procedure; others, of whom I was one, might go upon their own bent for days or weeks together. He neatly curtailed exploitation of his time by arriving every day just before one o'clock, so that to talk at length one had to forego lunch altogether, a demand that one's appetite generally forebade. At my original interview I had candidly informed him that my purpose in pursuing research under his direction was ultimately to apply the methods of plant physiology to ecology and I still admire the typical crispness of his remark that, whilst he appreciated my desire, he for his own part had found plant processes hard enough to explain when he had the subjects in the laboratory under controlled conditions, without undertaking the examination in the wild, where every factor of the environment might vary independently. I did not answer back.

It was a curious self-imposed test of one's seriousness that one should, if necessary, stay throughout the night in the laboratory so as to take observations for a crucial experiment. On one such night I explored in the small hours a little-used store-room for glassware, outmoded apparatus and such like, discovering to my astonishment a large portfolio of Victorian oleographs, depicting various races of domestic pigeons. They were of German source and almost certainly had belonged to Charles Darwin, having been stowed away here by his son, Sir Francis, who for many years had worked in the room opposite. This supposition was reinforced when I discovered a contemporary measuring glass with its ancient pontil break at the foot, and an intact sealed jar of specimens from the 'Beagle' expedition still containing original labels. The portfolio, so evidently relevant to *Variation of Animals and Plants under Domestication* published in 1868 was sent by Professor Seward to Down House to be added to the great collection of Darwiniana then in the custody of the British Association for the Advancement of Science. In the early 1920s Francis Darwin represented for us a strong link with the pre-war period. Though retired, he came into the Botany School with fair regularity, a tall and impressive, though ageing man, wearing a long snuff-coloured cloak and wide flat-brimmed hat. Plant material from the Botanic Garden was set out in his room by the senior laboratory assistant 'Henry' Elborn, together with simple apparatus devised some years before by Francis Darwin, who now busied himself with observations that were shortly written up for publication. It was however pathetically clear that the ageing scientist was in fact merely repeating work he had already done: it had indeed appeared in scientific journals and it was now the responsibility of the resourceful 'Henry' to secure the almost finished manuscript before it could be posted to an unsuspecting editor. This accomplished on one pretext or another, a new series of trials soon replaced the previous one. It all amounted to a kindly service to a respected teacher now losing touch.

Elborn was a great character in the notable brotherhood of Cambridge Laboratory Assistants. His long experience of the university and town had been enriched also by service in the Boer War and from him I learned much of the botanists with whom he had worked in the past. Of these none was more colourful than Dr Walter Gardiner, who happened also for some time to have been Bursar of Clare, where the senior clerk afforded me further insight into contiguous botanical and collegiate history. Gardiner was a botanical scientist of high distinction whose reputation specially concerned the proof that the protoplasmic contents of plant cells extended as very fine threads through the skeletal cell-walls, so conferring an effective living entity to the whole plant. This one could gather from the journals and one recognised Gardiner's eminence from his fellowship of the Royal Society. One now learned that Gardiner had a very deep regard for Queen Alexandra and each year celebrated her birthday by driving in morning dress to Cambridge station with a choice bouquet of flowers from the University Botanic Garden, and thence by train and cab to Buckingham Palace, where they were duly and dutifully presented. The courtesy was appreciated and when, in 1906, the new buildings of the Botany School were opened, her Majesty enquired for Mr Gardiner: he however had chosen to walk on the Gogs, in response to what impulse we have no notion. He was certainly now showing some oddness of behaviour, often rather disquieting. Thus he would apparently stroll into the Porter's Lodge from the College Bursary, absent-mindedly pick up the large poker from the hearth and continue his conversation while bending it to and fro, rather as one of the Russian emperors was apt to do. He was apparently very trusting of his lab-assistant, 'Henry', who would be appealed to from time to time by Mrs Gardiner to help quieten her husband. 'Henry' described to me, perhaps with elaboration, how being thus summoned to the Gardiner home, he found the master naked at the front door. Then the two of them sat amiably in conversation by the study fire, one naked and fondling a native assegai, and the other clothed and idly turning in his hands a heavy knobkerry until finally medical reinforcements arrived.

It now seems very likely that Walter Gardiner was responsible, during his period as bursar, for introducing into the Fellows' Garden of Clare the many uncommon species of trees still flourishing there, including the North American tulip-tree (*Liriodendron tulipifera*), the Caucasian *Pterocarya fraxinifolia*, the relict South European hazel, *Corylus colurna*, and perhaps also the Wellingtonia, *Sequoia gigantea*.

The general shortage of research appointments in the 1920s extended likewise to funds for apparatus, although in those pre-electronic days requirements were fairly simple, there was a general facility in glass-blowing (in which many students took practical instruction) and there was a respected tradition of building one's own apparatus from glass tubing, sealing-wax and miscellaneous hardware. Sometimes a research student would pay from his own pocket for a special component to be made, or exceptionally Mr Blackman might arrange for some item to be specially made at the Cambridge Scientific Instrument Company, with which organisation he was closely associated. It was this company whose expertise had allowed the building of a device then used by many of Blackman's students. It took the form of two precisely fitting brass drums like the halves of a large pill-box that acted as a gas-stream commutator. The glass tubing radiating copiously from it led to the nickname of 'Piccadilly Circus'. By its aid one could sample automatically at fixed intervals the carbon-dioxide output (or input) of any plant material under investigation, sustaining observation as required for days or even weeks. This was in fact being done in the laboratory to check the respiration of several types of plant material passing from maturity to senescence as with yellowing leaves or ripening apples. The apparatus was being employed to monitor the ageing of the evergreen leaves of the Wellingtonia when kept at a constant low temperature. The metabolic drift proved extremely slow and the carbon-dioxide output of the darkened leaves scarcely altered from day to day. Suddenly, however, the research student arriving as usual about 9 a.m. was astonished to find the sampling tubes choked with a copious precipitate of barium carbonate: after long quiescence, the leaves had evidently burst into a violent respiratory activity, a phenomenon totally new to us all. Its explanation came when the laboratory assistant disclosed that upon his earlier arrival, he had found the room smelling strongly of coal-gas, a consequence of a split rubber connection in the gas-supply to the thermostat. He repaired the junction, opened the windows, re-set the thermostat and left the experiment running as before. Only the massive precipitate in the series of 'Pettenkoffer' tubes remained to baffle the investigator, and to open up for him an unsuspected field of enquiry. Foolishly (although luckily, as it appeared) the air-supply being drawn over the respiring leaves had been taken, not from outside the building, but from the laboratory itself, so that they had suddenly been dosed with dilute coal-gas. It took little time to confirm that coal-gas could indeed affect plant metabolism in this remarkable way, and closer testing revealed that the major effect was due to a hydrocarbon gas, ethylene, that occurs in coal-gas. It was soon realised that these findings fitted the experience of the North American citrus industry where it was known that fruits stored in sheds warmed by oil heaters ripened and coloured far more quickly than those with hot-water pipes that were not thus (inadvertently) exposed to the products of imperfect combustion. Ethylene had been recognised in these products and before long this had given rise to the commercial practice of gas-ripening citrus fruit, in which a cargo of green fruit in its sealed rail-van is dosed with a given concentration of ethylene, to emerge at the end of its journey already three-parts ripe for the market. It is evident that the gas acts by accelerating the whole process of ripening, affecting the totality of the plant metabolism of which the respiration is a fundamental expression. Subsequently it was proved that the living cells of the senescing fruit or leaves themselves give off ethylene, so that the ripening process is autocatalytic, accelerating as it progresses. The implications for storage, transport and the general theory of cellular physiology are of self-evident importance, and it is amusing to contemplate the chance beginning of such a far-reaching enquiry.

Removal of the constraint of Tripos courses set the new research student free to make more flexible use of his time. He was generally asked to undertake casual demonstrating to first-year classes, either in botany or (for a shorter period) in plant biology for first-year medical students. This had the double advantage of providing a small additional income and of keeping one abreast of current elementary teaching. In my own case the junior demonstratorship brought me extended duties of similar kind. Not only had I to demonstrate to Professor A. C. Seward's practical classes throughout the three academic terms, but for each class I had to prepare a 'demonstration bench' of specimens of special appeal and current interest to the content of the lecture. To select and add to them I had to consult the Professor before his lecture, for he might choose to refer to them in the lecture-room also, or modify the explanatory notes I had given to accompany them. I came greatly to appreciate these contacts with Professor Seward not only for their botanical scope but for the first glimpses it gave me of his wise handling of the affairs of the department.

The beginning research student was now able to take extra courses such as mathematics, statistics (then just becoming generally applied to biology) or German, still the vehicle for a very large proportion of scientific publication. He was also free to resume or extend some form of games that would afford exercise in the flat and enervating countryside of Cambridge. My own desire to be out in the open chimed with my interest in botanical field-work, particularly a series of ecological studies at Wicken Fen, the extensive nature reserve lying within moderately easy reach of Cambridge. I was concerned to understand the processes of vegetational succession operating there and especially those concerning the establishment of bushes and subsequent formation of scrub and fen-woodland. As a basis for documenting the changes involved, during 1923 and 1924 I set aside, surveyed, marked and mapped two substantial areas of the Fen. Mr Tansley's private generosity ensured that the larger of these areas was securely fenced. Both areas have been subsequently remapped at intervals of some years, the larger most recently, in 1973. The value of these long-term factual records has been steadily confirmed in an area where 'an ounce of fact is worth a ton of theory'.

It is perhaps appropriate to notice that in 1923 we began research without benefit of a Doctorate of Philosophy in prospect. In Germany it was generally thought of as the hall-mark of research and our own distinguished men of science were plain 'Mr' for the greater part. This situation began to change after the first war, as was most apparent by the creation in 1925 of the University Board of Research Studies with official registration of research students for Ph.D. and M.Sc. degrees. The Secretaryship of this body was vested in R. E. Priestley (later Sir Raymond), geologist and antarctic explorer, who addressed himself with enthusiasm and vigour to the post. Elected to a fellowship in Clare, from his college rooms on E staircase he gave breakfast parties of amplitude and friendliness that soon brought him into personal contact with all students registered with the Board, a development valued particularly by the growing numbers of overseas candidates. It will be understood that in 1925 as a junior fellow in Priestley's own college I could not easily resist his argument that there was an obligation for me to submit a dissertation for 'his' Ph.D. This shortly followed, happily with the desired outcome.

Oddly enough, my external examiner for the Ph.D. was none other than J. H. Priestley, brother of R. E. and esteemed head of the Leeds University Department of Botany. I began the *viva-voce* in some trepidation but presently Priestley asked me to explain a term repeatedly used in the thesis, to wit 'onto-genetic metabolic drift'. It was a Blackman term not generally known in the current scientific literature, but familiar to us all from lectures, supervisions and discussions, indicative of the natural shift with age in the metabolism of every kind of tissue. Unwilling to take on the exposition of F. F.'s term before his face, I modestly said that I thought Mr Blackman would be a better expositor. To my delight my two examiners thereupon engaged in a lengthy cross-discussion of the term and its value whilst I recovered my wits.

This was only one instance of a phenomenon that has always impressed my imagination, the tremendous power of certain phrases or words, that from the moment of creation have such command over the imagination that they sweep forward to general usage and an applicability far beyond their merits. Blackman did this even more effectively when he invented the concept of 'limiting factors' whose power for seizing opportunities for misapplication proved to be such that its author told me he doubted whether he should ever have let it loose. In the theory of vegetational succession F. E. Clements had liberated another powerful beast when he wrote of 'pre-climax' or 'sub-climax', terminology that A. G. Tansley and I tried to displace by introducing 'deflected succession' or 'plagiosere'. It is somewhat daunting (even tempting) to encounter this factor operating in would-be scientific thought and I find that I resent the fashionable use of the term 'strategy' for an habitual pattern of behaviour in the life of a plant seeming to confer some benefit: thus 'strategy for survival, for multiplication, for pollination' etc. This is not permissible in logic because 'strategy' is a word applicable only to a deliberately conceived plan, a course of action designed to achieve a specific end. The usage complained of is an example of teleology, the false argument that explains plant or animal structures as contrived in order to carry out a given function or role, in short 'argument from design'. To say that the buds of the horse-chestnut are sticky in order to protect them against insect attack is just such an argument. The stickiness may or may not have the effect spoken of: this must be subject to observation and experiment, but it cannot be more than conjecture to say that the stickiness is there *in order* to give the protection specified.

Likewise we cannot conceive the plant as having designed a strategy to meet its needs although it may indeed have a pattern of inherited behaviour looking as if it might have. In the absence of information about the plant's intentions we had better abjure the term and retain scientific rectitude.

VII
THE NEW FELLOW

W H E N I became a fellow of Clare in 1925 the first range of the
Memorial Court had just been completed. The college had long
been pressed for space on which it might erect new buildings
but the river garden was so susceptible to floods that foundation
costs would have swallowed up most of the funds raised. We
had been forced therefore to consider building to the west of
Queens' Road, sacrificing the secluded Fellows' Garden, set
between those respectively of King's and Trinity. This was the
all-important opening move of the westward advance of
university and college buildings to be witnessed in the next
decades and it was fortunate that Clare chose so effective an
architect as Sir Giles Gilbert Scott. The preservation of the flat
wooded meadow land of the 'backs' rests upon a freedom from
intrusive building secured when Scott placed the all-important
building line of the Memorial Court along the crest of the gravel
ridge that flanks the river flood-plain to the west.

I had time to assimilate this possibility as, on Armistice Day,
11 November 1924, capped and gowned I stood with a mass
of scholars, students, fellows and visitors upon the wet lawn of
the old garden, to hear Lord Balfour, Vice-Chancellor of the
University, and the College Visitor, perform the opening
ceremony of the new court. It was then for the first time that
I heard oratory in the grand manner and appreciated the
quality of power in spoken English. The opening phrase was
so soon elaborated and so qualified that as clause followed
clause and ideas led from one to the next, I relinquished hope
that the logic or grammar could ever withstand such pressure.
At the time when all seemed lost, Balfour lightly tied together
the early gestures, summed up his theme and tossed it out to

us, fully resolved and complete. It was an architectural performance to equal Gilbert Scott's own.

By my election to a research fellowship in November 1925, I became part of a college body whose small size, at that time only some thirteen fellows plus Master, guaranteed a close and direct friendship such as is hard to imagine in these days when the fellowship is more than fifty. Six of the fellows were resident bachelors, and Priestley and I shared pernoctation in the Memorial Court, and when Harrison succeeded to the bursarship in 1927, he regularly stayed in college for dinner before smoking

Opening of War Memorial Court by the University Chancellor, Lord Balfour, on Armistice Day, 1924, with Sir Giles Gilbert Scott, the Master and Fellows: M. D. Forbes and H. Thirkill on far left: on the Master's left, J. R. Wardale, W. J. Landon, G. H. A. Wilson, W. J. Harrison and H. D. Henderson

a cigar in the Combination Room as prelude to bicycling back home to Great Shelford. In general we certainly took most of our meals, lunch and dinner, together in college so that opportunity for discussion of college affairs and entertainment of guests was ample.

The smallness of our numbers naturally meant a rather slow rate of fellowship recruitment since, although the Master would offer to qualified fellows the opportunity of accepting any vacant college living, few of us were in holy orders and so free to accept the kind, if meagre, offer. It was reported of the former tutor, J. R. Wardale, that, at the time of the death of the previous Master, Dr Edward Atkinson, in 1915, the infrequent chance arose for fellows and their friends to inspect the Master's Lodge. Two ladies were understandably transfixed by the half subterranean kitchens, where cockroaches scuttled over the damp flag-stones to shelter behind the massive cast-iron cooking-stoves and the gloom was relieved only by glimpses of sky at ceiling level. Wonderingly one lady confided that she thought that with such conditions for his servants, the fellows must have found it very hard to keep any Master. To which the Tutor, recalling that the college had only had two Masters since the battle of Waterloo, replied with resignation, 'That hadn't exactly been our difficulty'. William Webb had been elected on 20 July 1815 and Edward Atkinson on 14 January 1856, and Wardale had no doubt long abandoned the once-reasonable hope that he himself might have succeeded to the mastership. It is scarcely surprising that in the later years of his office, Dr Atkinson's discharge of his magisterial functions would some-times waver, as it was said to have done upon the admission of Mansfield Forbes to his fellowship. Undeterred by the almost ridiculous youth of the young man kneeling before him, hands together between his own, the scene in the College Chapel failed for once to elicit the operative phrase, 'Auctoritate mihi commissa, admitto te in socium huius Collegii' but launched him instead into the similar ceremony familiar from his days of Vice-Chancellor, of admitting this unlikely lad into the degree of Doctor of Divinity. The latinity and alertness of the attendant fellows were happily such that so unfortunate an ecclesiastical outcome was prevented.

The impact of age likewise disclosed itself in the next Master, Dr W. L. Mollison who had been a fellow since 1876 under the college statutes of 1861. I soon discovered as junior fellow, responsible for the minutes, that in the close air of the Combination Room, the Master would doze off whilst the Tutor ably directed the meeting of the Governing Body of the college. This in no way prevented Mollison from voicing a bitter complaint about the legibility of the hand-writing in which the baby fellow had set out the minutes: it was some satisfaction that the crabbed Aberdonian visage was turned equally harshly against whoever the scribe might be. Mollison had nevertheless suffered ill fortune in Clare since his mastership was marred by a fatal accident to Mrs Mollison on the service staircase of the Lodge, and it had also embraced so much of the tragedy of the First World War. The Senior Fellow at the time of my election was the amiable cleric, W. H. Fulford, who still retained the familiar name 'Fluffy' conferred on him by generations of pre-war undergraduates to whom he had been Dean: like the paired ponies at the horse-show, it made an inevitable chime with the name of his colleague, now Master, but then assistant tutor, 'Molly'. Fluffy, first elected in 1877, had returned with his family to Cambridge after a time at Abingdon in the living of St John's, Oxford. He was a figure made for the generation of college stories and before long I was to witness two of them. The first occurred in the Combination Room shortly after Christmas, when in reply to a query from Mansfield Forbes as to what kind of a vacation he had had, Fluffy replied that all was satisfactory saving his failure to get his customary greetings-card from Manny. In total serious innocence Manny replied that as he had been so very busy, this year he had only sent out six hundred! It was no use being chagrined to be listed 601st among Manny's friends for they went up into the thousands.

I had to wait a little while before collecting my second story of Fluffy, in fact until returning to college after marrying in the autumn of 1927. Fluffy kindly congratulated me and wished us good fortune: then assuming a contemplative and retrospective mien, he allowed that 'honeymoons are very nice in their way, but after a few days a man longs for a little intelligent conversation'. Fifty years later I am still at a loss to know the reply I should have made.

Naturally enough, Fulford was not now active in the formal running of the college, and its former tutor, J. R. Wardale, was rarely able to leave his home. Less senior in the fellowship by eleven years was H. M. Chadwick, University Professor of Anglo-Saxon, a lovable bucolic-seeming man with a soft Yorkshire accent and beyond doubt the college's most distinguished scholar. In 1922 he had married Norah Kershaw, a pupil in his own field of research and likewise a scholar of the utmost distinction: together they contributed a wonderful partnership ideally exhibited in their great three-volume work *The Growth of Literature*. Their command of linguistics was such that they modestly apologised for having failed to consult quite every one of the original sources in their world survey. By 1925 'Chadders' came into college only for demanding college business; all else, including the Faculty Board minutiae, gave place to the needs of teaching and research. Thanks, however, to our links with Manny Forbes, Fred Attenborough and various archaeological students, we happily kept close touch and contrived to hear most of the vivid stories that arose round him. Most durable and characteristic was the account of Chadwick's meeting in the former University Library at Goldsmith's Building next the Senate House with a small group of visiting Americans. Wishing to consult a volume in the reserved section of books in the central room Theta, they sought help from the kindly-looking industrious tweed-clad scholar at work near the door. Chadwick put down his notes and, in view of the difficulty of describing the route, conducted them to their goal, explaining the lay-out and pointing out features of particular interest. Eventually back at the entrance door they took a courteous leave, the American feeling in his pocket for a half-crown to offer to their guide. To which gesture Chadder made gentle reply of such quality as one that stimulated Sheridan to remark that he would almost rather have said that than have written 'Paradise Lost'. Chadder smiled and said in his soft Yorkshire voice, 'No, thank you very much: my employers don't allow me to accept gratuities.' The only word for it is 'delicious'. Chadwick's erudition was immense and his memory wonderfully exact and far-reaching: the fact that in his own field he was the unquestioned world authority could never persuade him that his students or his guests might not be better informed than himself. His rejoinder to one's inept or mistaken replies was a gentle 'I expect you know'.

Fred Attenborough had been Chadder's research student before becoming fellow of Emmanuel: he married Samuel Clegg's elder daughter, Mary, and they made a visit from my old head the opportunity to bring Sam and Chadder together. Not surprisingly I found Sam delighted by the quality of the Professor's personality: he explained to me next day 'What is so amazing, Harry, about Chadwick is his profound IGNORANCE'; he paused, and added, thoughtfully, 'Ignorance, I mean, compared with the average secondary school teacher!'. Chadwick once unboastfully confided that he thought he had never forgotten a date that he had once heard: a condition unimaginable to most of us.

Leaving aside the most senior fellows, the special case of Chadwick, and myself, the unfledged apprentice, there remained the central body of experienced fellows on whom the effective well-being of the college depended. There were the two categories, not altogether separate, of the college officers (the Tutor, the Bursar and the Dean) and of the 'Official Fellows' who were dons of such weight and experience as to take responsibility in the college for some major branch of teaching, such for instance as classics, mathematics, engineering or medicine. Alternatively they might hold important university office. Since the size of the body was then determined by the number of separately endowed fellowships, only a modest list of subjects was thus covered although the college had 'gone outside' for new fellows to meet its needs in engineering, divinity and classics. Even though undergraduate numbers were small, only a modest proportion of them were supervised by fellows of Clare and many, perhaps most, went for this service to members of other colleges, not necessarily fellows, who were glad to undertake the work in supplementation of a low college, university or free-lance income. At this time, the middle twenties, university posts were few and ill-paid (my own demonstratorship being worth £90 per annum) so that supervision, casual demonstrating and examining offered a welcome measure of support whilst seeking foothold on the academic ladder.

Likewise, of course, colleges had not the funds (nor was it thought needful) to provide official teaching fellowships to give teaching cover on the present generous scale for all sections of undergraduate examination work. Instead, in managing the college there was a dual concern, on the one hand to keep an eye lifted for any vacancy likely to appear in the fellowship numbers, and on the other, to recognise and cherish any young graduate, especially of Clare, who might possess such outstanding academic promise and acceptable personality that to secure him as colleague would be a significant gain, no matter in what academic field he might chance to have specialised. The college thus aimed at long-term security and distinction whilst providing at the same time an entry into an academic career where alternative support, even for the ablest, was scarce indeed.

In 1925 the college Bursar was G. H. A. Wilson, a mathematician from Geelong who in 1927 became University Treasurer under the new statutes of 1925/6. It was evident that this post took less time and energy than it afterwards acquired, for Wilson devoted each afternoon to a country walk with his spaniel *Brin* and each evening to bridge with the Master of Caius and other friends. The slight difficulty of keeping a dog in college was overcome by the Governing Body through the simple expedient of deeming Brin to be a cat. He was not, however, entitled to a yellow ribbon round his neck like the majestic black feline that had for so long traditionally decorated the Court and suppressed kitchen-dwelling rodents. Wilson served from 1929 to 1939 as Master of Clare and was University Burgess just before the suppression of this mode of representing the university in Parliament. Upon occasion the forcefulness with which he expressed himself lent colour, not to say excitement, to college business. Having brusquely complained to a certain university office, Wilson was said to have demanded the reason for delay in answering, only to be told in trembling tones by a fresh voice, 'I'm sorry, sir, Mr X has fainted'.

W. J. Harrison, who succeeded Wilson as college Bursar, was also a mathematician, employing his expertise as one of the original boffins of the First World War in solving gunnery problems. He was characteristically methodical and extremely hard-working and it was said of him that when as a student he left to begin his Tripos and a friend wished him luck, he replied, 'It's not luck I want: I want my deserts'.

He had to operate as Bursar within the very limiting rule that colleges might not invest in Equities, and their holdings in land and property were controlled by consent of the Ministry of Agriculture. Even so, it was largely Harrison's wise rearrangement of college property within the given constraint that provided the financial means subsequently to complete the Memorial Court. His dry wit enabled him to keep at least on level terms in the verbal fencing that Priestley so much enjoyed. The latter, as Secretary General, had introduced a university scheme whereby a 'Composition Fee' became payable by students taking certain aggregate courses and it occasioned a good deal of comment. Priestley reported over dinner that he gathered that the body of the bursar of Trinity Hall had been discovered under a deep deposit of correspondence on his office desk. 'What would you have done, Harrison', asked Priestley, 'if *you* had found him like that in your office?' At once Harrison replied 'Oh, I should certainly have charged him a *de*composition fee'...and would have collected it from the General Board, no doubt!

After P. C. T. Crick had left for his Australian see, his place as Dean was taken by another Clare mathematician, Will Telfer, who went on to take orders and had thus served in France as Chaplain for a large part of the war, gaining the M.C. In his college office his kindness and deep sincerity earned everyone's affectionate respect, returned servicemen and freshmen from school alike. He had a great sense of humour which Priestley tried to exploit when, after dinner, Telfer was due to say the concluding grace. If Priestley was at the head of the table he would tell his funniest story and at once stand up to end the meal: Telfer, though congested of visage, happily always controlled his voice.

I myself recall how in the beginning of the Second World War, during the deep improvised black-out, three soldiers had been killed by a lorry through having thoughtlessly walked homewards down the line marking the road centre. I asked Telfer what hymn he supposed the men had been singing on such an unwise path: with only the slightest hesitation he said he supposed it must have been 'Brief life is here our portion'.

From what I have already written it will have become evident that Raymond Priestley exerted a good deal of influence in shaping the administrative structure of the university during a time when great changes were involved through the adoption of the new statutes of 1925–6, firstly with the Board of Research Studies and afterwards as Secretary-General of the Faculties, a post carrying the responsibility for running the General Board, one of the three senior administrative bodies of the university. Since this body was that primarily responsible for all matters of teaching and research, it was certainly no disadvantage to Clare to be so close to the executive centre. Wilson was soon to become University Treasurer and Henry Thirkill, first as Tutor and later as Master, displayed constantly increasing skill and aptitude in the widest range of elective university representation. For all its small size Clare accordingly came to have something of a reputation for administrative know-how, and it was interesting to realise how this was reflected in the activity of J. W. Landon, Clare fellow in engineering since 1919 and Secretary from its inception, of the new Faculty Board of Engineering, a body of such width of scientific cover that within its own walls and by its own staff it provided the lectures and practical classes to cover the full three years of a Tripos course for a large body of undergraduates. To handle this organisation from the beginning required a man of both character and scholarship, as indeed Landon was. In Clare the impression he made upon me was of wisdom and far-sightedness with constant encouragement for cooperation between the scientific and humanistic interests within the college.

The linkage of extraordinary scholastic accomplishment and highly eccentric behaviour is exhibited more commonly in Oxford and Cambridge combination rooms than in less sheltered environments and it could hardly have been more evident than in A. D. Nock who came to us as a classic from Trinity in 1923. It was soon apparent that he had a mind of the most formidable retentiveness and the college grew used to the flying visits of scholars from even the most distant places who sought Nock's opinion or recollection of sources of information. To save time he limited such visits to an afternoon walk when, on the Coton footpath, he would be asked about early religions, peoples or histories, always being able at once to give the volume and generally the author and page of a named source in the learned periodicals or books where the information was to be found. The delighted investigator thereupon returned to Pekin, Cape Town or Munich having saved himself much labour, for Nock was proved invariably correct. It was not surprising to his Clare colleagues that Nock quickly made himself master of the regulations governing payment of income-tax, and he was swiftly engaged to look at the drafting of the new statutes of the college then in preparation.

THE NEW FELLOW

It was Nock's misfortune to be extremely hypochondriacal and he gave the Bursar considerable trouble investigating imaginary risks in his college rooms. On one occasion, working in Istamboul he noticed the unclean drinking glass at the next table and imagined that this and his own had been infected with venereal disease by the unsavoury customers. He shot back to Vienna to get competent medical advice, but this being entirely contrary to his personal view that he was already at great risk, it was disregarded and he returned to Cambridge and the comfort of his own General Practitioner who reassured our *Malade imaginaire* and even forbade him possession of a clinical thermometer, since he knew that Nock could elevate the obedient mercury merely at will. The fact that Nock took his more impressive guests to dinner in Trinity was not lost upon the small society of Clare and in fact he seized the opportunity in 1930 to accept the offer of a Chair in Harvard, where he built a high and deserved scholastic reputation, welcoming his former colleagues from Clare with great generosity, flapping his gown at them in expansive gestures clearly copied from the repertoire of the famous histrionic Cambridge don, J. T. Sheppard of King's.

Of the three remaining places on the college body, one was occupied by a fellow of some standing, who made my first meeting of the Governing Body both painful and memorable. He had become so irascible and uncooperative that the fellows had regretfully decided that he could not be continued in his college office and he had been told that he would not be re-elected. To my horror the fellow concerned made a point at the meeting of developing a lengthy 'explanation' aimed solidly at me, on the grounds that I had not heard his side of the argument. It disclosed, of course, strains that so small a body could not sustain, and lacking the *savoir faire* to abstain, I supported the rest of the fellows in the vote that followed. It was feared that public disruption might have been carried into the sexcentenary celebrations shortly to be held, but happily this did not happen. I remain grateful that never again did I have to experience so emotive a college meeting: no doubt also the apprentice has toughened his hide with time.

The only other members of the fellowship in 1925 were the Senior Tutor, Henry Thirkill, and his neighbour on F staircase, Mansfield Forbes: they both were figures who made so great an impact upon the life of the college and entered so much into my own growth within its walls, that it has seemed appropriate and fair to give space to separate comment upon them.

As now, all the fellows with the Master jointly constituted the senior college authority, the Governing Body, which dealt with elections to fellowships and college offices and all important general issues. Small though this body was in 1925, its work was supplemented by the statutory body, the smaller College Council, which dealt with the day to day running of the college, especially all its teaching functions, and it was built around the official fellows regularly involved with them, that is to say, the Tutor, the Dean and the Bursar. These were supplemented by the other official fellows and one or two more annually elected. The Council met often and was expeditious and convenient. In the fifty years or more that have since passed, increased affluence based *au fond* on changed national and university attitudes, have led to great changes especially in numbers. There are now between fifty and sixty fellows in the college, all members of the Governing Body. This has made it inconveniently large for many purposes, but it obtains no relief by making alternative use of the Council, since this also has become very large, chiefly because a considerable part of the fellowship is now made up of college lecturers or university teaching officers, categories of fellow entitled also to a seat on the Council. Thus what used to be a relatively quick, intimate and informal manner of discharging college business has become far more a matter of committees, sub-committees and reports, the familiar price, indeed, of success.

VIII

NEW COURT

DURING MY THREE YEARS as research student I had lodgings near Parker's Piece where the nearness to the laboratories was a great convenience and the smallness of the rooms was compensated by the great kindness of my motherly landlady Mrs Howard. My bedroom on the first floor was the dimension of the hall below, so narrow that, whilst large enough to hold the single bed and the chest-cum-dressing table, side by side, there was barely room for drawers of the chest to open. Length was likewise curtailed and in bed in the summer one stretched one's feet luxuriously on the sill of the open window.

It was a great contrast moving to the fellow's set of rooms in the Memorial Court. I bade farewell to the sad oleograph of the Cameron Highlander *Absent without leave* who was now under arrest by the bedside of his dying father, and embraced the prospect for the first time of furnishing my own living quarters. The basic provision was indeed luxurious, with separate entrance hall, telephone, gyp-room and toilet, a well-proportioned sitting-room with built-in book-case, cupboards and fire-place, large dining-room, bedroom and adjoining bathroom. Taking occasion of the visit by my former headmaster to his daughter in Cambridge, I was able to draw on Mr Clegg's experience and taste. On an excursion to the London shops I was introduced to the excitements of Heals and acquired dining-room furniture of 'limed' oak appropriate to the natural wood of the rooms, and this was followed by a visit to an old friend of Mr Clegg's in the Liverpool Street area. This was an Armenian carpet merchant, Mr Benlian. I was treated to a professional display of bargaining that ended, when agreement seemed unlikely, in my acquiring a few glowing Hamadan rugs that were to give continuing pleasure over many

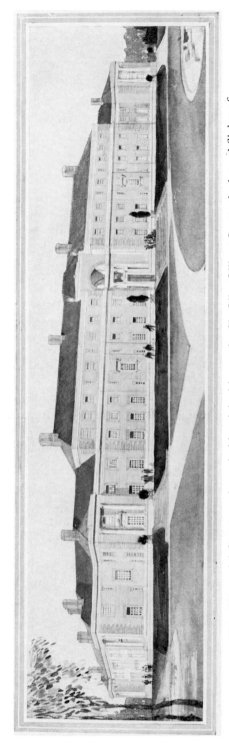

Clare Memorial Court, as shewn in his original layout by Sir Giles Gilbert Scott: the lateral flights of steps were not used

years. Railway posters done by Paul Henry and Medici prints took key positions on the walls, whilst leisure and service were provided by substantial plain hide-upholstered settee and chairs obtained at advantage from the midland town of origin: they remain serviceable if shabby fifty-seven years later. I claim a little indulgence in thus describing my first set of rooms since it was to be the centre of my college life until after the end of the Second World War and became very familiar to generations of friends and students from Clare and elsewhere.

During 1914–18 the tremendous flow of war casualties had been met in the Cambridge region by the discharge of hospital trains at a large sidings next to the Long Road at the south side of the town. Thence the wounded suffered the uncomfortable transportation to the large temporary 'Eastern General' hospital that had been built on the Clare–King's playing field, the lovely cricket ground where now the University Library stands. The cessation of the War was followed by such acute housing shortages that throughout the country 'squatters' took possession of any premises temporarily becoming vacant and this is what happened to the wooden huts of the Eastern General Hospital which indeed suffered such occupation until the building of the University Library offered a reason for repossession of the site so strong that it could not reasonably be refused. In 1925 the families occupying the hospital site enlivened the scene beyond the Clare boundary fence by looped lines of coloured washing hung out to dry and air. The pictorial possibilities encouraged me to attempt to cut a colour woodblock of the scene from my sitting-room but it was not very effective and I turned instead to representing the Real Tennis courts visible beyond the huts and framed by shapely trees. Here variation of the autumn sky in the hand printing of the blocks made an acceptable series of variants in the product. My interest in wood-block printing had been sustained by my friendship since undergraduate days with Frank Kendon of St John's who, after war service with the Friends' Ambulance, was now engaged under G. G. Coulton in research on mural paintings in English churches. In the book he afterwards published he ventured the conjecture that the medieval spread of printing and the associated black line wood-block illustration, were the likeliest means by which travelling artists promoted their craft of mural decoration. He readily learned the simple form of wood-block cutting that I had practised at school and in return introduced me to the techniques of wood-block engraving with the burin upon the polished end-grain of box-wood, a process allowing reproduction of fine detail and only recently being superseded by half-tone printing in the commercial publishing trade.

Life in my new rooms was exceptionally comfortable and one came to accommodate to minor flaws in building design. The windows proved to be set too far below ceiling level, creating a heavy belt of shadow, a fault avoided in the later range of buildings. The set of the rectangular block transversely to the prevalent westerlies meant that the wind seemed to strive to get through the great archway and, failing that, rushed through windows, doors and crevices throughout the building so that no position remained in the bed-room where one had refuge from the blast on its way from the sitting-room, over one's legs to Queens' Road. Lt. Col. Barham, who provided the money for building one of the two corner staircases of the new court, laid down the requirement that there should be a yearly service on Armistice Day, held in the Memorial Gateway and at which should be sung either Kipling's 'Recessional' or the hymn 'The strife is o'er, the battle done'. Thus at 11 a.m. on 11 November for many years the College held a religious service centred upon the placing of a wreath of Flanders' poppies beneath the bronze plaque of the names of the fallen that occupies the inside wall of the arch. In what I now think a priggish light-hearted way, I complained to Telfer that the line from 'Recessional' – 'Lest we forget, lest we forget' – seemed to have a hint of blackmail in it. Perhaps scenting blasphemy, even unintentional, the Dean promptly banned Kipling's hymn and henceforward our services had no choice.

In later years the service has ceased, which I find a matter for regret: perhaps I am too moved by the recollection of the deep hush that, on those earliest Armistice Days, fell across the whole landscape as the exploding maroon at eleven o'clock signalled the two minutes' silence, with all traffic along the Backs at a standstill as the multitudes of war dead were, in real reverence, for a while remembered by their survivors.

The purposes of the fellows' sets in the Memorial Buildings were several. To begin with the statutes laid it down that the research and official fellows had entitlement, subject to consent of the Council, to select vacant rooms for their occupation. The new buildings, of course, partly met the extreme limitation of space in the Old Court. It also went a long way towards solving the problem, becoming more serious now that fellows were more often married men, of finding fellows to pernoctate, to sleep in the new court and to be responsible for keeping order there. For a great many years and long after my marriage I fulfilled this duty as part of my obligation as a fellow 'to best of my judgement and ability' to 'discharge the business of the College which may be entrusted to me'. Over a long period of time the pernoctation was shared by two of the fellows: to begin with it was Raymond Priestley to whom every morning I waved from the bathroom across the archway space, but during the Second World War it was our close friend Dixon Boyd, Professor of Anatomy, with whom sharing was made simpler by the fact that he (and for some time his family) lived in our home as part of the war-time transfer of the London Hospital staff and students to Cambridge, when the severe demand for space led to such expedients as the dissection of cadavers at the top of the Sidgwick Museum of Geology.

I had enjoyed a term or so of ease in my comfortable rooms when I was slightly surprised to be reminded by the Tutor that it would be not unreasonable to undertake some supervision for the college: doubtless to soften the prospect, he told me that in the new academic year he had coming to college from Uppingham a particularly attractive student already addicted to botany and a well-informed field naturalist. Thus began a long and happy association as pupil and colleague with John Gilmour, who was to become in turn Assistant Director of the Royal Botanic Gardens at Kew, Director of the Royal Horticultural Society's Garden, Wisley, and, from 1951, Director of the University Botanic Garden in Cambridge.

The intention of supervision within individual subjects was a discharge of the all-over College responsibility for tuition that had progressively been assumed by the university system of organised lectures and practical work. As college supervisor one would see each allocated student in a class of two, three or four (more seldom singly) for an hour each week at which one discussed all the problems raised by the week's work, discussed the essay prepared for the class and already marked, and considered any general issues raised by oneself or the men. Especially one sought to fill in the gaps in botanical science left by the lectures, and to erase the errors or misconceptions that even Professorial teaching can engender. Many men came up with very little knowledge of the old-fashioned principles of classification of flowering plants, although ability to use a flora was assumed: here was a gap one could help to fill and the Memorial Court provided at hand populations of suitable material for improvised field instruction, not least the great elms, afterwards alas victims of Dutch elm disease.

I always aimed to aggregate men of similar status or ability, and so to manage the class that they actively pursued the logic of argument and evidence for themselves. It never worked better than in an *ad hoc* group consisting of three men respectively from Clare, Selwyn and Peterhouse, all quite first class. Of them the Clare man, G. C. Stevenson, became a plant pathologist employed for a long time in Mauritius; John Turner as Professor in Melbourne played a very considerable role over many years in the development of botany in Australia; and Nigel Balchin was the very able and esteemed author and playwright whose writings so perfectly reflected the manner and speech of this country in the years before and during the Second

World War. In these classes no holds were barred and every subject under the sun was mentioned. John Turner and Nigel Balchin indeed developed a much cherished friendship with the family, and one which led us to informed detail of the intimacies of undergraduate life undreamed of by the average don. Nigel had attained his education at Dauntsey's School by way of a 'Kitchener' scholarship for sons of men wounded in the First World War, and to comply with a condition of studying agriculture, he found himself in his third year constructing experiments in field labour on the University Farm: thence he advanced to experimental and industrial psychology, the area which is so well illuminated in his writings and which *inter alia* led to the creation of the long-enduring and profitable invention of the selection of chocolates, 'Black Magic'. It is gratifying to consider my living-set on N staircase as background for the generation of such friendships, aside altogether from the instruction taken so much for granted.

We were separately paid for all college supervisions at rates generally agreed by the colleges. It was hard work, especially as it involved careful marking beforehand of the essay preparations set for the week. Not less than fifteen or twenty minutes would be so spent for each man, and as I undertook eight or ten classes per week the total was formidable. Formidable even when the students were male. However I came under great pressure, hard to refuse as Demonstrator in the Botanical Department, also to supervise students for Newnham and Girton. I settled to take a weekly class of twelve or fifteen and this proved Herculean labour, for they were hideously conscientious. Each of the women students turned in two essays, and each essay was at least twice the average length of those of a male student. The marking alone took hours and when the class met me in the small lecture-room at the lab, it would *not* utter. It sat, poised to write down what I might impart, and resisted solidly all my efforts to get anyone to venture an idea or opinion: the give and take of controversy and argument on the validity of expressed opinion was not, it seemed, for them!

Winter sunlight on Clare Bridge and Avenue

I guess that the essays must have provided me with plentiful subjects for exposition and amendment, for the demand for the class did not decline.

With the loss of their private garden beyond Queens' Road, the fellows now made more use of the river garden, and on warm summer evenings took out the odd wooden 'cheeses' to play bowls on the lawn or improvised a form of soft-ball cricket that was, alas, rather destructive of the borders. To a botanist going along the avenue several times a day, it soon became evident that the trees of common lime, *Tilia europaea*, which composed it were very far from uniform. They consisted of three distinct populations of differing ages. The oldest and largest, planted when the avenue was constructed, had huge clear trunks and massive branches, attaining a great height, possibly ninety feet. In the intermediate age-generation the trees were smaller in size, both girth and height, and had clearly been planted in gaps opened up by local deaths of the older generation. The third generation was of trees, still at the original spacing, but much smaller then the older series, sickly and shedding their branches. Oddly enough the youngest were the weakest and gaps grew as they died and were not replaced. The key to this domestic problem in arboriculture was offered to me by our evening cricket games, where search for the tennis-ball showed that right along its length the north flank of the avenue was supported by a solid red brick wall standing up four or five feet from garden level. On the south-facing side the avenue stood next to King's Ditch and here the corresponding brick wall was far deeper, possibly eight or nine feet. Thus the two walls enclosed a raised causeway between the river bridge and the stone gateway fronting King's Pieces. The lime trees were thus planted inside a kind of giant window box whose soil had not been replenished for two centuries or more. The first generation of trees flourished admirably, but whenever age or disease made a gap in their regular rows, the replacements had to make what growth they might. The massive skeletal roots of the older trees were at hand to put their new feeding roots into the vacated plot and, facing such competition, the new-comers never reached the dimensions of their predecessors and many of them died early. As the avenue grew ragged again, further replanting made matters worse, and the condition of the third generation of limes was so poor that they have since been removed. Happily several of the noble giants of the first planting have been left and lend great dignity to the prospect of the avenue. Reconstruction of the history of the avenue would have been more difficult today for G. H. A. Wilson, bursar when the Memorial Court building was in progress and at a loss to dispose of the excavated sub-soil, ordered it to be dumped all alongside the north flank of the avenue, where it hid the retaining wall beneath a wide bank of gravel that has only been made fertile by much effort from the gardeners. The width and the lateral position of the bank have cost the avenue much of its former architectural quality of a narrow raised viaduct from the Old Court across the strip of low land liable to flood.

Along the north side of the river garden, shielding it alike from inclement wind and the gaze of the curious along Garrett Hostel Lane, is a high wall of pleasantly weathered Cambridge brick. Then as now it supports on its southern face unusual flowering shrubs and climbers that luxuriate in the high midsummer temperatures, but on the opposite northern face it was backed in the 1920s by a closely set row of very tall elms that extended the full length of the garden, providing it with a notably impressive backbone. When one penetrated behind the wall, there was the Garrett Hostel ditch bordered and overhung by flourishing yews twenty or thirty feet tall and underspread with ivy. Between the heavy-foliaged yews and the tall columnar elms was a secluded gravel path where in the crepuscule one might come upon the Dean in quiet perambulation. At one point the exotic snowdrop-tree (*Halesia* sp.) had been planted, its pendant white blossoms suggesting to me that to reserve all the underplanting to white and preferably scented flowers would enhance the solemnity and dignity of the ' Dean's

Walk'. This has in fact been most successfully accomplished, the effect even overriding the later felling of all the elms.

This dreadful excision was a consequence of the extensive spread of Dutch elm disease in the period before the Second World War, when, since coal was scarce in college, it was arranged that undergraduates might saw up the felled timber for their own use as fuel. In this way all evidence of the great line of elms disappeared. We were never again to see, as a result of an abnormally frost-free spring, the river garden so crowded with self-sown elm seedlings that the gardeners had to hoe through the flower beds to be rid of them.

Botanists may however comfort themselves that the river

Warren's wrought-iron gates (c. 1713–15) reveal Grumbold's bridge and the west front of the college

garden provides for them specimens of two fine exotic trees, as it happens oddly similar in habit to one another. The longer-established is a swamp-cypress, *Taxodium distichum*, a native of the Everglades in Florida, in whose black swamps it produces its woody aerating roots that protrude into the air from the submerged root-system. Perched upon the drained river bank in the Clare garden, these structures are absent, but we can see its elegant habit, the larch-like foliage shed annually as feathery twiglets and the tiny round pollen-bearing cones falling in considerable number. Some years after introduction of the swamp-cypress, we planted in the wet centre of the garden a sapling of the dawn-cypress, *Metasequoia glyptostroboides*, a species known in ancient fossil state but regarded as extinct until rediscovered in 1945 by an expedition to a remote region of China. When introduced to the gardens and arboreta of many

The Master's Garden, seen from the Lodge across the river to the bridge, the avenue and river-garden

parts of temperate Europe and North America it has proved to grow with great vigour and this has been typical of the tree in the Clare garden, as of others planted elsewhere in Cambridge.

I have written in this Chapter primarily of the events and scenes associated with my earliest years in the Memorial Court. There were great changes to come, various colleges were to follow our example and build new courts across the Cam, the University was to create the Sidgwick Avenue centre for the Humanities and, most imposingly in every sense, Sir Giles Gilbert Scott entrusted by the university with the building of a new library, was to place it, almost to an inch, upon the axis of the Clare Memorial Court, and finally this court was itself greatly extended in those further episodes beyond that which initiated it in 1925. In the 1920s these manifold developments were only to be guessed at.

IX

HALL AND COMBINATION ROOM

To go over from one's rooms in the Memorial Court for dinner, to lunch or college meeting in the Old Court was, in architectural and visual terms to step backwards from the twentieth to the seventeenth or eighteenth century: the Combination Room, the comfortable centre of the common life of the fellows was itself served by the staircase arch that bore the date 1688. Hall, Library and Combination Room had all been laid out in line astern to take up the full length of the court at first-floor level, and when the intervening doors are thrown open there is an imposing view from the stairway entrance in the Master's Lodge right through to the neatly placed college Arms set axially at the east end of the Hall. One finds it a little surprising that these arms should be of cast-iron whilst their design speaks at once of Jacobean or Stuart wood carving.

In 1925 the Combination Room shewed its superb proportions and fine windows, with beautiful late Stuart panelling in reddish oak darkened with linseed oil and dust and spoiled by tall book-cases standing where they transected the lower part of the panels. The fire-place had its wonderful carved oak soffit polished by the shoulder-blades of generations of fellows who had stood on the heavy fender to warm their stretched trouser behinds in front of the log-fire. The panelling was surmounted by a noble carved and gilded cornice, as good as any in Cambridge; it had been seriously threatened some years earlier, by a fire in the floor above it, the so-called 'Warren', but the damage had been repaired by an excellent local craftsman, old John Whittaker.

The general impression of the room was none-the-less stuffy, hot and ineffective. Tremendously heavy crimson curtains depended from opulent curtain rings and rods that totally spoiled one's view of the cornice, the floor was covered with a preponderantly red Persian rug of such dimension that it was reputed to be a legend in the village where it had been specially woven, the fireplace had cheeks of blue and white tiling far less appropriate than the cast-iron 'Sussex' now replacing them, and the furniture embraced a mahogany table so highly polished by Webb, the butler, that it had normally to be preserved beneath its baize cover. The table was flanked by sabre-legged chairs, again of dark mahogany, of immense weight and uncomfortable width. What however set strongest seal upon the room, especially outside daylight hours was the central lighting fixture, a tremendously heavy-looking bronze colza-oil lamp cast so that its several arms supported a ring of incandescent glass bowls, now converted to electricity. This structure, possibly five feet across, swung in the room centre, directly flooding one's vision so that maximum discomfort was attained. When once the fellows had tried the experiment of indirect lighting from standards little time was lost in banishing this fitment to storage. It certainly merited conservation, not only because colza was the locally grown fuel of the Fenlands, but also because of the intricate art nouveau castings of ivy and acorns that scrambled in profusion all over its surface. The Victorian aspect of the Combination Room has been enshrined in three photographs reproduced in the *Clare Book*, especially that shewing tables ready laid for the sexcentenary luncheon given on 13 July 1926 to H.R.H. Princess Mary and Viscount Lascelles.

When the fellows were persuaded that modification of the Combination Room furnishing was overdue, they sensibly avoided dispute among themselves by taking the advice of Mrs Edward Maufe, then acting as consultant for Heals. New blue velvet curtains were hung so as to reveal the cornice fully, the dark Regency chairs were reupholstered in blue leather and before long the Persian rug, now sadly worn in the doorways, was replaced by a fine Chinese carpet. I remember being surprised and satisfied by Mrs Maufe's choice of redecoration

The Combination Room laid for the Sexcentenary Luncheon, 1926, given for H.R.H. Princess Mary and Viscount Lascelles.

of the ceiling in soft unemphatic pastel colouring. Of the original lighting of this fine room there was no remaining sign. I favoured then for it, as I still do, silver sconces set on the oak panelling, just as one may see in the central block of Hopetoun House near Edinburgh, where the late seventeenth-century panelling is of almost exactly similar character. However, nothing in the academic world is harder to agree upon than the lighting of the communal rooms, and a delay of half a century or so is only to be expected, saving possibly a specific bequest of some happy argentiferous benefactor.

The fellows mostly dined in Hall, seated at the High Table in order of seniority under the daunting gaze of Hans Pfeiffer's immense wooden caryatids whose ostensible purpose was that of placing a wreath over the stone bust of Elizabetha de Clare where it surmounted the mantel. Pevsner laments the subsequent loss of this triple edifice: few who were overlooked by it will do so. Lunch (and dinner in vacations) was taken in the Combination Room and at either meal we had fellows' guests as well as a good sprinkling of those M.A.'s with dining rights, particularly those who were regular teachers for the college: they jointly imparted great variety, width of experience and wit. We had at this time no resident fellow in law and made much use of H. T. Ll. Roberts, a prewar law coach for the college, both doctor and lawyer with much experience of the Far East and of Russia. He was a portly and amiable man and excellent raconteur; his anecdotes included a horrifying one of tommies on leave in Aden taking a rowing-boat into the harbour and trying (as they reported) to spoon up on their oars the active yellow-striped 'eels' swimming in the surface water: happily they failed to lift upon the floor-boards even a single specimen of this deadliest of all sea-snakes! H. A. Wootton, an old Clare man had returned from the war to be head-master of the Perse school, and had an equally horrifying history to relate. As research chemist in the later stages of the War he had been concerned with the trial development of that appalling liquid, Lewisite (mustard-gas) and he recounted how he went to Avonmouth, measured the stuff in a laboratory glass cylinder and poured it directly by hand into the waiting rows of open shells standing on the dock. One could hardly better this as an illustration of the immaturity of scientific technology in the First World War. Close to my own interests were those of A. H. Evans, who, a classics coach by profession, was also a considerable field-botanist, and secretary of the local committee of management for Wicken Fen. He suffered from *Locomotor ataxia* and would engage the assistance of undergraduate helpers such as John (J. S. L.) Gilmour and Jimmy (J. M.) Scott to collect his more prickly and inaccessible rubi (blackberry) variations for him.

I seldom was able to disengage his lunch-time conversation until we reached King's Parade, where he set off from the Senate House for Bowes & Bowes with arms and legs flying like windmills to the dismay of the local traffic. At a far more distinguished scientific level was C. G. Lamb, Reader in Electrical Engineering, a fine pianist and also of such eminence as an entomologist that he had on this count received his University Doctorate in Science. He was extraordinarily kind to the raw young don but when I learned that he had been one of the founder members for the Society for Psychical Research and broached the subject with him, he turned abruptly away declaring that he only discussed this subject with those having several years' experience of it! Intuitively I ignored this display and reshaped my enquiry, and was vouchsafed then a sequence of admirable comments from one of detached scientific judgment who had been personally involved with many of the great investigations in the early days of serious enquiry into the paranormal. I well remember him saying, as he lent me a wonderful early publication by one of the pioneers, that I should discover that in this area of research, every succeeding generation would only be satisfied by its own newly-collected evidence: this of course is true enough, and is indeed highly understandable.

Among those who most frequently came to dine at the High

Table were fellows of other colleges with special ties of affection for Clare, such as the zoologist H. H. Brindley of St John's, world authority on the cockroach and one time companion of the great yachtsmen, Erskine Childers; and Sir William Hardy the pioneer biophysicist. Brindley had unbelievable powers of recollection on subjects as diverse as the genealogy of the nobility, the rigging of mediaeval sailing vessels and the quirks of university personalities. Over the years I never knew his conversation to fail or to be repetitive, and as I often travelled back in the *Fenman* from London with him, I found it a convenient rule to introduce, as the guard's whistle blew, some suitable theme of my own choosing, for it was a certainty that Brindley would expound this topic, with interest and skill, until the train slackened to a stop in Cambridge. Brindley supervised all the Clare men reading zoology, and stories about him were legion. He was the kindest of tutors to me in small-boat sailing on the Norfolk Broads.

For a while at the Fellows' Table we enjoyed the company of E. Alfred Jones who was elected to the status of Fellow-Commoner so that he could more conveniently compile the authoritative catalogue of the College silver, subsidised by Paul Mellon and nobly published in 1939 by the University Press. Alfred Jones had an unchallenged world reputation in this field of descriptive and analytic recording of historic Plate and the interplay of his sensitivity and wit with those of Manny Forbes greatly enlivened the board. I specially recall the phase when both of them, at a pretended loss for a word, would refer to any conceivable object, topic or person as a 'document', a technique extending confusion widely.

None of the resident M.A.'s with dining rights in college had a more distinctive personality than 'Billy' Drew, a contemporary and friend of G. H. A. Wilson. After a period teaching in public school he had returned to Cambridge and a career as teacher of singing at what one could fairly call 'consultant' level. Since we were close neighbours in the early 1930s, we had frequent opportunity to experience both his sensitive musician-

'Manny' Mansfield Duval Forbes, 1924

ship and his authentic and caustic wit. I remember with
continuing relish his reply to a query by his wife, Sybil, as to
the colour she should use for the respray of a second-hand car
she had recently been given. Billy, already bored to tears by

endless chat about the 'new' car, finally said 'I should paint it white-elephant gray'. My mind still fails to visualise any such colour. One supposes Billy Drew was a match even for the prize wits of the lower school. Facing the query 'How long would the gas in a fairly large gasometer last a fairly large town?' he reports that he said 'Oh, a fair time in winter and twice as long in summer'. Billy was to be feared as a wit but greatly to be admired as teacher and singer. One evening Sybil had filled the big studio of the 'Oast House' with a rowdy party enjoying the contemporary dances of the time and she had the misfortune to ask Billy, tired and head-achy, if he would please *sing* to them. One could feel how affronted he was, but he sat at the piano and sang for them the old ballad of 'Lord Randall'. His light but superbly controlled voice stilled all the noise of the gay party, and the deep sadness of the ballad fell like a pall across the room. The wet-blanket was swiftly felt by everyone as a rebuke, despite the beauty of its performance.

I have mentioned only a small sample of the many scholars and teachers whose devotion to the college made them so valuable a support to the very restricted capacity of the small body of fellows. Without college fellowships or university positions for the most part, they did not regard themselves as deprived of 'rights' but cheerfully sustained themselves by college- or school-teaching in its many forms, taking pleasure in the many amenities and facilities of a scholastic environment. Some certainly flourished thereon. Thus when I was responsible first for teaching plant-biology to the big first M.B. (medical) classes of the post-war years, I was able to draw on the services as demonstrator of C. Warburton, whose research had been decisive in solving the massive problem of the wide transmission of trench-fever in troops along the western front. Warburton had kept his stock of experimental animals, human fleas, in small pill-box containers with gauze lids, so that, removed on schedule from the warm comfort of his waistcoat pocket, each colony could in turn be given pasture upon his wrist, allowed to feed through the gauze whilst the box was safely held by an elastic band. Not surprisingly there were many stories in circulation of accidents at feeding time, and of losses sustained at dinner parties, with all the brouha-ha of the hunts for recovery. Needless to say this did not involve the trench technique of pursuit of strays by a hot candle-flame run along the seams of underclothing.

Warburton's bright bird-like figure was long a welcome part of the Cambridge scene, and when he attained his 100th birthday he had just won a national crossword competition. Replying to the toast at the party given for him by fellow-villagers at Grantchester, he replied to a query as to the secret of his own longevity by the suggestion that he thought 'most people simply gave up trying'.

The fellows of Clare were for the most part bachelors living in college; or if married they held posts from which they were readily available. So they took meals regularly together, making use of the opportunity to retail items of college business. Of the body of fellows none made more decisive impact than Mansfield Forbes who had been elected in 1912 from a background as historian, but subsequently lecturing and teaching English with enormous effectiveness. In appearance he was extraordinarily juvenile and puckish with straying fair hair, thick-lensed round spectacles bound up by an ancient pipe-cleaner, and, for much of the year, irrespective of the conventions, he wore ragged mittens drawn down to cover his wrists. His small acute features were at once thoughtful and inquisitive, so that oddly enough there was a touch of both angel and monkey in his look. Always engaged in enthusiastic support for some idealistic concept, usually with social implications, he pursued Judge Douglas's 'Trial Marriage' concept and the 'Hundred New Towns for Britain', explaining them in his own rich and allusive vocabulary. When the college decided that celebration of its six-hundredth year called for celebration beyond the Royal Visit, the fellows had little hesitation upon settling for a Memorial Book illustrative of the college's history, and Forbes was unhesitatingly made editor, and, as it turned

Grumbold's seventeenth-century staircase tower above the kitchen
passage that lies behind the north range where it overlooks the
back-premises and horse-chestnuts of Trinity Hall

out, almost exclusive author. The fish thus hooked was massive, and altogether more (certainly better) than had been bargained for.

It is difficult to imagine the consuming enthusiasm with which Manny embraced his task, the staggeringly long hours of research and writing he devoted to the job or his endless pursuit of helpers. His historical training and his visual aestheticism led not only to tracking down of fine old photographs of the college, but to the commission of fresh pictures to allow *Country Life* to exploit views and contexts of college life that no one else had somehow noticed. He involved J. F. Greenwood, a north-country miner of particular promise, in making wood-engravings of the Avenue and Old Court, and Sydney W. Carline in creating pencil drawings of the college roofs from unexpected angles. He wrote typically of these explorations as shewing themselves to be 'true Clare country, well dowered with relevancies of delight as well as sustenance'.

What complicated and threatened all along the line to frustrate Manny's undertaking was what was then acknowledged as his 'perfection-complex', an impulse that forbade him to stop whilst he might still explore every last ramification or qualification imaginable. On and on the writing hastened, and as the Long Vacation term began, the fellows were displaced from the Combination Room by tides of Manny's notes, correspondence, illustrations and references too numerous to be confined to the Library or his own rooms. By the next Michaelmas Term compression had become painful and the original volume, swollen in size, had now become two. The proofs it is true, looked marvellous, but in the end a halt had to be called to scriptorial passion, and ultimately, as often turned out, Telfer and the junior fellow collaborated with Manny in closing a reluctant last chapter. Before this had been achieved another casualty littered the path. Manny, heavily pressed for time and due to take his holiday in Scotland found it essential to continue work in his native land, and failing transport of several volumes of the Dictionary of National

Clock, belfry and oriel windows of the inside of the Old Court shewn
from above the chapel archway

The College Avenue shewing the cathedral-like quality of the still intact
lime-trees

Stone shell-hood over the entrance to the Chapel archway, a feat of great
and unexpected delicacy

Biography requisite to him, carefully tore out small sections of
the D.N.B. to take along. As the fates decreed, Wilson, then
Master, also needed whilst Manny was absent, to consult the
same entry or entries and discovered the dreadful outrage,
made far worse by the fact that the perpetrator was himself the
Librarian! 'Quis custodiet?' indeed, the Master enquired and

Queen Anne period staircase in the Master's Lodge, one of the finest of
Cambridge stairs

Manny, despite elaborate and even faintly rational excuses, had
to relinquish his librarianship.

Once again the violence quietened and in the interests of the
college and our affection for Manny, continuity of the
production was sustained so that in the end two volumes were

printed, vastly larger and more expensive than had been forecast, but of superb quality and together providing a monument unmatched among colleges.

Whilst the Master and Manny found each other irritating and inconsiderate, Wilson had more sympathy than most of the fellows for the visual aesthetic sensibilities of Manny: each conceded this common ground and Wilson not only made something of a hobby of drawing but was a successful collector of English Georgian drinking glasses, which on ceremonial occasions in the Lodge were set out, several at each dining place, admirably playing up to the handsome college silver. Indeed later on, when Gordon Russell reintroduced the commercial marketing of hand-made 'Georgian' glass, it was easy to persuade the college to buy and use this to supersede its own spindly-shanked Victorian glass-ware that sat so poorly on the heavy oak tables in hall.

Now is scarcely the time to write of the Fellows' Library, for although it is a fine room designed to carry shelving exclusively on the walls, at this time it had been filled and over-filled with the free-standing two-sided oak 'classes' and the corresponding one-sided banks of book-shelves transferred thither, one supposes, when the pre-existing library was demolished, with the early chapel below it, at a time in the mid eighteenth century. These classes were constructed in 1626 among the earliest of open-access shelving in Cambridge and were themselves of excellent design. Now however they were filled to the eyebrows, stacked in close rows, with disordered miscellany upon their upper stages and dusty piles of transactions and papers closing access at floor-level. The floors were indeed bowing under the load, cleaning and consultation were virtually impossible and we waited impatiently for opportunity to set it all to rights.

I had been asked by Manny to lend him a hand in preparing for the *Clare Book* his account of the woodwork of the college, that is to say, of the Old Court and I found it a task of consuming interest, involving repeated discovery of unsuspected felicities and links with college history. A great wealth of panelling was still to be recognised and described, some transferred from buildings still standing when the Jacobean court was being erected and perhaps suffering some ill-judged tailoring or even burial below the wall-plaster for two or three centuries to come. Most of all however the Old Court was now recognised to hold such wealth of staircases of varying age that it provided examples of the evolution of the domestic wooden staircase through 'the long renaissance century the College took in building'. Newel-posts, finials, pendants, balusters and hand-rails all exhibited the robust and functional virtues of good oak joinery, from the early newel stair to the fine elegance of the wide and gently-rising stairway in the Master's Lodge of which Forbes wrote 'few wooden staircases in England surpass this specimen in grace'. The satisfaction I had from my exploration of the woodwork itself was very greatly enhanced by the affectionate competence of the account in which Manny's English welded my own findings to his own wide experience of decorative architecture and collegiate buildings.

I have written above of the vivid and kindly personality of Manny Forbes as it affected me in my earliest years as scholar and new fellow in the college, whilst he was still living in college rooms. There was a later phase when, in 1929–30, my wife and I shared residence with him in his home at 'Finella' on Queen's Road, when this had now become the effective centre for his evangelistic support for the visual arts, and a refuge from the distractions of life on a college staircase. Of this more anon.

X
COLLEGE TREASURES

CONSIDERABLE PART of the great charm of living in an ancient university such as Cambridge lies in the circumstances that one is surrounded by the visible evidence of the piety and generosity of scholars and patrons who were one's predecessors. The chapel service for commemoration of benefactors, in Clare is repeatedly punctuated by the generous refrain 'and Samuel Blythe', and one could not have more satisfying preface to a college foundation than our wise and imaginative launching by Elizabetha de Clare. The record of benefactions reminds us of the endowment of fellowships, livings, prizes and such comforts as an occasional feast or brazier in Hall, but more constantly in evidence than these are the buildings themselves, the books, silver and pictures, many of them linked immediately to known individuals and particular phases of college history. Such objects and structures, not seldom also of singular artistic quality, constitute a heritage that demands conservation as well as augmentation, and the record of both processes is apparent as one lives in the college environment.

I recall particularly the very hot dry summer of 1921 when I spent the Long Vacation term in the Old Court, all that then existed, and saw from the oriel window above the entrance gateway the brown rectangular markings of buried foundations intersecting the green lawns. These were the traces of that older court of Clare that made way for the new early Jacobean front in which I was then living. The same drought disclosed on King's College lawn the pattern of all those houses between Milne Street and the river that the King had taken over to make space for his new college. At the time of those early Clare buildings the mediaeval chapel stood on the present chapel site, but occupied the ground floor of a two-tiered structure with the college library above. It was from this library that, as the new frontage was built, the college transferred the lovely oak classes made around 1625 and housing upon their open shelves the precious books that it had so long been customary to keep chained up. When the northern range of the court had been completed after the interruption of the Civil War, the classes suffered more than two centuries of inappropriate crowding and darkness in the Fellow's Library but when finally transferred about 1947 to the Forbes Library on the ground-floor of E staircase, they were seen to sit there serenely, each double-faced class occupying space between two windows, being fully lit from both the north and the south face. Surely the mediaeval library must have followed just such a pattern, nor need we suppose that the sooty wall of Trinity Hall kitchens then occluded the northern face as it later infringed on the mid-Georgian chapel windows.

When the student population returned to college after the First World War attendance at Chapel was still obligatory. One found the building of that time crowded with pews and overwhelmingly sombre. This was especially so on entering through the ante-chapel where from the marble floor one feels a strange under-water sensation induced by the singular cold lighting from the octagonal cupola high above one. The Chapel was very dark, not only from the undistured soot gathered on ceiling and walls, but more especially because of the deplorable mid-Victorian stained-glass windows that occupied every opening with dense colour, reducing the body of the building to a dark cavern: of this the editor of the *Book of Clare* could only advise 'a downward gaze in the search for better things'.

A few years later the fellows, taking courage, removed most of the Victorian glass, leaving one obscure original in the far north-eastern corner, backed by the blackened rear wall of Trinity Hall. This is an environment that makes a bad window worse and demonstrates how dismal the fully glazed edifice must have been. The opposing south-east corner still has the

Chapel interior, shewing the wonderful response to replacement of
Victorian stained glass and extensive cleaning

other relict Victorian window, a gift from a one-time fellow who was University Librarian, and although more transparent than its congener, none-the-less still rather daunting.

Thus about 1939 the window apertures were now filled, apart from the two instances mentioned, by a clear greenish glazing with narrow leads holding small geometrical panes, a typical Hanoverian style, to the prodigious improvement of the whole chapel, particularly when accompanied by cleaning and restoration of the pale wash colouring of the coffered ceiling. The pattern and tints had been most carefully recorded at the exploratory cleaning by the architect Harold M. Tomlinson, who, after strenuous service in the Fleet Air Arm during the First World War had joined the staff of the University department of Architecture. At first a member of Christ's, he subsequently joined Clare and built for the college the two highly successful lodging-houses 'Castlebrae' and 'Ethelreda'. He and his pupils designed several tasteful dwelling houses for Cambridge people, but the stresses of early flying from the heaving decks of battleships at sea took unfortunately early toll of him.

The aesthetic improvement of the Chapel evoked, as was perhaps foreseeable, unease that in the process some of its religious quality had been lost. The designer, Hugh Easton, was accordingly commissioned by the Governing Body to prepare sketches for a new replacement window to go in the south-western corner of the Chapel. The cartoons were spread on the Combination Room carpet, amendments were discussed and some accepted. The outcome was a considerable success, the completed design representing Richard de Badew, the founder, presenting Our Lady with a prototype of the first collegiate building: the whole a luminous aerial pageant, the principals attended by fat cherubs in the conventional decorative Georgian style. In the corner is the elegant trademark of Hugh Easton, incorporated into the lettered arms of a weathercock. The same signature confirms the origin of a very similar window in one of the side-chapels of Durham Cathedral, where its delicate conceits are no match for the daunting power of the great Norman columns standing solemnly around.

Not long after the first, a second Chapel window was installed which however had been too hurriedly commissioned. It represents the crucifixion, the figure of Latimer and the chapel at Little Gidding, and seems to me to carry the deliberate affectation of high Georgian design to a point that is repulsive in such a solemn context, not least offensive in a curly red caterpillar contrived of descending droplets of blood! Such hazards and successes of design are a natural part none the less of the evolution of our college buildings that in stone, wood or glass alike reflect the very human qualities of our changing society.

It will be apparent how strongly evident in the post-war period of the 1920s still was the generous hand of Victorian benefactions alike to Combination Room, Hall and Chapel. Still more widespread was yet another influence, dirt.

The use of household coal for heating and cooking all through Victorian and Edwardian time created great defilement of college buildings and an incrustation of sulphurous soot gathered over the cream-coloured oolite except only where exposed to driven rain or constant downwash. When, after the Second World War the college was able to embark on a programme of extensive repair and restoration, and coal-firing had been replaced by gas heating, prominent in the proposals for restoration was cleaning of the stonework. About this time it had become generally fashionable, notably in London, to remove the surface soot by jet-washing, usually behind builders' screens of tarpaulin: this was sometimes supplemented by steam treatment. These processes were regarded by some of the college body as inherently hazardous to the fabric, a hypothesis confirmed when, during washing of the Senate House exterior, water seeped inwards along the masonry joints, inducing an alarming fungal growth on the interior panelling of the building. We were already aware that the wide exterior string courses of the Old Court often provided ledges on which rain and snow collected, thence seeping into the walls. It was accordingly decided to eschew the use of water in favour of a slower but safer process of hand-scraping and brushing, a treatment that extended in the next few years round the entire court, fully restoring its pristine loveliness. Deep rotting of the limestone was found to be largely restricted to the balusters: several of these, especially in the north-western corner where they regularly were bathed in black swirls of smoke descending from the kitchen chimneys, were heavily corroded on the faces sheltered from the cleansing drive of the rainy west winds, i.e. especially below their own bulbous overhang. Such balusters were wholly or largely replaced, as also were occasional fractured blocks of stone elsewhere, a process made possible only by the Bursar's fortunate location of a small but sufficient residual outcrop in the quarries from which the stone for the court had originally been drawn.

The drying out of wet walls unprotected by adequate damp courses had been successfully applied to the fabric of Versailles and whilst in Finella we had seen McGrath completely dry out, by the use of inserted porous ceramic pipes, brickwork hitherto dripping with water. This technique the college now used to dry out the ledges on the walls of the Old Court: happily it was fully effective. The enthusiastic competence of the Bursar in due course ensured also the overdue restoration of roofs and refurnishing of window-sashes and frames by teak, far more resistant than deal to decay and in no need of painting. These sustained if costly remedies have restored to the court a wonderful freshness and charm. I seldom see it on a spring day across King's lawn, or enter through one of its gateways without unconsciously expecting to encounter, as I have done so often in the past, the slender graceful form of the Master of Trinity, Lord Adrian. He would confide to me that he was introducing his week-end visitors to the loveliest of all college buildings, Clare Old Court, and I would reply with perfect truth that I myself was in process of solacing myself and my own guests by sight of the only other possible contender for this title...the

Great Court of Trinity. Were it possible to have enlarged the respect and admiration I have always held for this peer among Cambridge scholars, his shared devotion to the beauty of Clare would have ensured it.

Nothing is more speedily identified as part of the 'treasures' of a Cambridge college than its collection of silver plate, objects beautiful in themselves and certified by the Latin inscriptions of their donors as part of collegiate and indeed of national history. The first meals I took in Hall as a raw and wondering freshman introduced me to the charm of the college silver, nor have I since lessened my appreciation. College numbers were then so small that it was customary to make use each evening at dinner of much cutlery and small silver plate all decorated with the college crest and engraved with the name of the donor. Drinks ordered from the buttery came in solid Georgian tankards or in straight-sided Victorian beakers of uncommonly attractive proportions and a surface broken by engine-turning in a fine basket pattern. When one had attained the dignity of the High Table one could more closely examine the standing pieces, salts, cruets, cups and covers etc., and at conclusion of the meal the butler brought to the head of the table one or other of the two pairs of basin and ewer. It might be the handsome rococo pieces of 1739 given to the college by Henry Clinton, Earl of Lincoln, or the plainer pair made to the order of the college in 1770 from the silver of three tankards given by three former fellows of the later Stuart time, their tankards no doubt much used, their commemoration was now transferred by the inscription of the remade plate a custom of great civility though liable to cause some confusion. Rosewater was poured into the dish which was passed along the table, and the fellows each in turn dipped the corner of his napkin and used it to wipe his lips and behind his ears where the 'alderman's nerve' awaited grateful stimulation. Raymond Priestley was fond of insisting that fellows of Clare might always be identified by the whiteness below the ears. I have neglected to determine the situation with the Fellows of Trinity where the same ceremony has now become vestigial, the Head of the High Table shaking his head sadly in rejection when each evening the butler offers him the rosewater ewer and dish. What a delightful Ph.D. subject!

On the special, though infrequent, occasions of feasts we enjoyed the spectacle of seeing the Hall entirely lit by silver candlesticks, for happily the great sooty clusters of batswing gas-burners that used to nestle like bat colonies near the ceiling had long been done away with. The multiple point-sources of mellow candle light waver continuously and reflect in innumerable surfaces of cut-glass and polished silver. This is incomparably the best means of illuminating the hall and renders ridiculous such schemes as those which guarantee to provide easy reading of *The Times* at every seat, and which might indeed well attain the utter flatness of a cinema foyer! We are happy in Clare to have available silver candlesticks sufficient to light the entire hall and to provide illustration of the changing fashion of candlestick design from the Restoration onwards: the wealthy Whig fellow-commoners of the Georgian period saw to it that this finest period of silver craftsmanship was fully represented. They could hardly do less in face of the gift to Clare in 1744 by Lord Ashburnham, First Duke of Newcastle, Vice-Chancellor, persistently Prime Minister and one of the wealthiest men in the country. The magnificent cup and cover that he presented was the work of the great Huguenot silversmith, Paul de Lamerie (1739–40). Authoritative opinion has it that this is 'the finest example of Rococo silver at Cambridge', although we also possess three other fine Georgian cups and covers whose dignity and restraint are at least equally appealing. Of these three the most ornate is the 'Pelham Cup', by the famous woman silversmith, Eliza Godfrey, 1745/46.

Handsome though the Georgian plate may be, one must admit at once our oldest silver to be the seal-matrix presented to the college by our Foundress in 1359. It is carved in intaglio with the figures of Elizabetha de Clare giving the charter of

Founder's Seal, given to the College in 1359 by the Foundress,
Elizabetha de Clare

foundation to the Master and Scholars. Too soft to be regularly
exposed to the pressure of seal imprinting, the original has been
replaced by a more durable, although less handsome version for
day to day use, kept in a suitable safe under the Keys of the
three 'chestkeepers' prescribed by our Statutes. One cannot
resist the speculation that for a very long time the original seal

had its home in the prodigiously heavy pine-wood chest sheathed in iron that still sits, incongruously, in the centre of the Fellows' Library. It has wrought-iron handles that can be lifted to take the strong pole needed to move the chest, and one may still see beneath its closed lid the three separate strong locks that had to be opened together by the three fellows that in mediaeval time acted as chestkeepers like their present-day successors.

The seal-matrix apart, we have in Clare no examples of Founder's or other very early silver such as, on occasion, graces the High Table of Trinity Hall, Corpus Christi, Gonville and Caius, Christ's and Pembroke Colleges. For one reason or another these failed to reach Charles I's Royal Treasury at Nottingham and thus were preserved the lovely mediaeval salts, mazers, cups and horns that so excite our admiration. Special circumstances however did ensure the preservation in Clare of a handful of pieces from before the Civil War. These mostly came to us from Dr William Butler, the celebrated and fashionable doctor who was physician to King James I, and who for some years had been a fellow of Clare. There is a group of these vessels all made in the middle of the sixteenth century: they were made respectively in Germany, Holland and England, and are known as the Poison Cup, Falcon Cup and Serpentine Cup. It was only after repeatedly setting them out on exhibition that it became clear to me that these vessels were part of the shamanistic apparatus of the great physician, since they were all associated directly with the detection, storage and nullification of poison: they would have made a handsome display for any consultant's sideboard. The conical crystal in the lid of the Poison Cup is supposed to turn cloudy with the presence of poison in the tankard, the 'Serpentine Pot' is turned from a rock alleged to neutralise poisons and the 'Falcon Cup', which is not a cup at all, is the hollow effigy of a hawk, the bird anciently associated with medicine, concealing two secret compartments, the one the pedestal on which the bird stands

The Poison Cup, one of three items of plate with a 'consulting-room' aspect given to the college by Dr Butler. The lid carries a rock-crystal said to detect poison and the other revealed when one removes the hawk's head by the nearly imperceptible join at the neck.

Upon his death in 1618 Dr Butler left money to the College and instructions to have made 'a very substantial fair communion cup of the most purest and fine gold that can be found'. This, with its associated paten was taken by Dr Barnabas Oley to the King upon the outbreak of the Civil War: they were redeemed by him and brought back to the vicarage at Great Gransden where legend has it that they reposed in the duck-pond until the Restoration. They thus became the only such objects of pure gold known from this period in England, and they are, as well, vessels of remarkably serene beauty.

After Charles II had come to the throne, gifts of plate were again freely made, although now in the prevalent style of deeply repoussé silver-gilt, a mode well exemplified in the Chapel alms-dish, probably a secular piece made over to chapel use and heavily clustered with the winged heads of cherubs and the swollen blossoms of tulips and other vegetation. The dining table was now also graced by a fine large silver-gilt tankard and a smaller but very lovely silver-gilt cup-and-cover.

With the opening of the eighteenth century the silver collected by our gifts began to display that simple purity of form, beauty of surface and elegance of engraving that for me at least make them unrivalled. The soft metal has yielded to constant polishing from the butler's fingers and I am always reminded that the silver trade of Sheffield employs for the ultimate polishing of their best wares only the delicate skin of the forearm of its women employees.

I will not engage on survey of the riches of our Georgian plate, nor express regret that the silver of Victorian and Edwardian origin is thinly represented, for by these later times the inspiration of designers and craftsmen was enfeebled and misdirected. By the early years of the present century the influence of Morris and his followers was already being felt in reconsideration of the principles of many ancient crafts and a number of Cambridge colleges became patrons of artists of the new persuasion. I recall how very impressed I was on first seeing the fluted

rosewater dish and ewer designed for Corpus Christi College by
R. M. Y. Gleadowe, art-master at Winchester and subsequently Slade Professor at Oxford. Thereafter I pressed my own
college to expend its next suitable benefaction on a commission
by a modern designer rather than upon addition to examples
of older plate. We were well rewarded by the silver fruit-tazza
and bowl designed and executed for us by C. J. Shiner in 1937.
Happily a similar patronage has been so expended that pieces
by several leading silversmiths now worthily accompany our
older treasures. These artist designers include besides Shiner,
R. H. Hill, E. G. Clements, J. Warwick and A. G. Benney:
their contributions have the special historical appeal of commemorating events of our own time. Thus in 1934 we were
presented with a heavily rimmed plain silver tun bearing the
arms of Clare and of Trinity Hall on opposing faces. It closely
resembles the Founder's Cup of our neighbour college and was
given to us to mark the occasion when, during reconstruction
of their own kitchen, we fed them, in a quasi-biblical manner,
by a large hole cut through the wall between us.

We were greatly encouraged to acquire modern silver by
Professor R. S. Hutton, the first Goldsmith's Professor of Metal-
lurgy in the University, who became a fellow of Clare and was
afterwards Prime Warden of the Goldsmiths' Company. He did
such sterling work (if the phrase is allowable) during the War
in preserving the Company's ancient Hall and contents from
the dangers of the London blitz that the gratitude of the
Worshipful Company, forbidden to repay Professor Hutton
directly, found expression in the gift to his college of a suitably-
inscribed coffee-pot designed by R. H. Hill. Accompanied by
sugar bowl and milk-jug *en suite*, it proved an extraordinarily
successful design, and through a good part of the next few years
it was away from home at national and international exhibitions
of contemporary British silver.

A third piece with the strongest collegiate historical linkage
is the water-jug designed by James Warwick and given to us
in 1950 by Mrs Chadwick in memory of her husband, Hector
Munro Chadwick. The vessel is chased with deeply fluted ocean

waves over which sails the Viking ship illustrated on the cover of du Chaillu's famous book, a work that turned 'Chadder's' formidable scholarship permanently to this field of study. *Ad hoc* commissions of this character, on whatever scale, prove a most attractive means of acknowledging amity towards the college alongside the sustained inflow of traditional pieces by donors recognising the evident suitability of special items, such as the choice selection of early spoons given by A. C. D. Pain, a notable oarsman and boat-captain of the early twenties, the tea-service of 1788 given by the Revd F. I. Wane, and the magnificent kettle and stand of 1761 presented by Mrs Wardale in memory of her husband, J. R. Wardale whom I recall meeting as my tutor in 1919. I can still see him with sparse white hair and perched spectacles searching the trunk below his study table for the correspondence that would identify this fresh Clare man.

There is also a very special sentiment that attaches to two heavy silver mugs designed by A. G. Benney and presented by the College in 1961 to two of its most faithful servants, as gyp Arthur G. Galer since 1924, and as bedmaker his wife, Minnie, since 1927. The college has also expressed its benevolence towards the artist craftsman by commissioning designs by R. H. Hill and A. G. Benney for the two 'Greene' cups given annually to incepting Bachelors of Arts respectively for 'general learning' and 'regularity of conduct'. This enlightened sponsorship is agreeably in the vein of R. S. Hutton who would have liked to see a competent young silversmith paid to pursue his craft before the University in a studio workroom at a centre such as the Fitzwilliam Museum. His views recalled to me Sam Clegg's much earlier suggestion that the University would do itself great credit by similarly sponsoring some established British artist where he could be seen at work and could make easy contact with those in university of any rank who might be interested in the visual arts. We might well, with Rendle Harris, quote the 'Eastern Proverb' – 'The dogs bark but the caravan goes on.'

XI
DOUBLE HARNESS

It has always been very advantageous to combine a university post with a college fellowship, and in the years directly after the First War this was especially so because of the meagreness of university stipends. Now that in 1926 I was made Senior Demonstrator in Botany, my annual salary became £90 per annum. However the increased security given by the post together with the research fellowship and the completed doctorate, was excuse enough to embark on marriage. Financially the hazard was less than seems apparent, for the largest part of the income was to come not from the sources mentioned but from fees for supervision, for casual demonstrating and for the setting and marking of examination scripts. In the marking of school examination papers in botany and biology, my wife, also a biologist and science graduate, shared the load. It would, none-the-less, be idle to pretend that we were comfortably off, and a quick summary of cash assets when we returned from our honeymoon revealed a total of just over two shillings. It was also very fortunate for us that on the expiry of my research fellowship later in the year, the college saw fit and was free to convert me into an official fellow.

Opposite Pembroke College, and connecting Trumpington Street with the riverside, runs Little St Mary's Lane, where my wife and I went to live in the first year of our marriage, 1927. We occupied No. 6, a tiny romantic cottage directly fronting upon the narrow pavement from which the post-man or baker could easily hand up deliveries through the first-floor sitting-room window. This room, reached more conventionally by a steep narrow stairway, gave us a prospect of the oldest of existing college facades, the north front of Peterhouse, and afforded a grandstand view of the labours of a famous though ageing geometrician, Dr Lackland, who, in earth-encrusted carpet slippers, excavated the ancient tombstones of the grave-yard of the church, piling them into small random banks of varying lithology to constitute a disorderly and discontinuous rockery instead of the onetime relative order of the railed-in burial enclosure. The daily help of our next-door neighbour to the west took much pleasure in the summer display of flowers and rejoiced us by her Malapropisms concerning them. She preferred, as she confided, the 'antirhiniums' because 'they are so profligate'!

Next door to us on the east was the house of our landlord, N. Teulon Porter, a character of some notoriety in his day and landlord of the 'Half-moon' a one-time inn now without a licence but still displaying an exterior hanging sign and interior fittings based on half-sawn barrels as seats, oaken boards, and shelving for vessels carrying such witticisms as 'There is soup in everything'. Teulon Porter was a man of striking appearance, with heavy torso but lower limbs damaged by some earlier accident or by polio: he held forcefully to 'advanced' sociologi-cal views, especially on the importance of sexual psychology and the need for more widespread knowledge of contraception. His open willingness to promote these views in the student population led to the women's colleges placing their ban upon the 'Half-moon'. No doubt encouraged thus each Sunday morning opposite our windows a deep fifty-yard bank of female bicycles stood stacked deep against the graveyard fence whilst their owners enjoyed the hospitality of the former inn. So far as we knew, Porter held no college or university post, but avidly sought and achieved the company of university teachers and proponents of views similar to his own. He naturally did not lack detractors, but many young people, such as our Indian research students, felt that he was something of a public benefactor.

For our part, my wife and I were outraged by the rent our landlord charged for the tiny property and the very meagre secondhand contents that sufficed to classify it as 'furnished', and we left at the end of the year. Perhaps we were helped by an unannounced visit by the Master of Clare. One day when I was working in the Laboratory the portly Dr Mollison struggled up the creaking stairway to the minuscule sitting-room, and after the usual polite preliminaries announced to Margaret that we should certainly have to leave, since 'your friends will not come to see you here'! Indeed we had room for only a small gathering and the large, much decorated hats then worn by senior Clare ladies entangled all too easily with our one ceiling light fitment. None-the-less we had a deep affection for the terrace cottage overlooking what we regarded as our own churchyard garden, as had all the succession of young honeymooners that in turn held its tenancy.

Margaret and I still recall nostalgically that during our brief tenure of No. 6 Little St Mary's Lane, our favourite niece, then a school-girl, was left in bed one evening in the attic bed-room whilst we kept some prior appointment in the town. Upon our return a startled little voice announced that in our absence she had been visited by a man standing in the lane, looking up towards the light and repeatedly calling for GOD: we had no difficulty in recognising this as Manny's call-sign for me (a convenient abbreviation). The child, less familiar with the local language, solemnly told us that she had not replied and we did not blame her at all.

About this period there was a strong social obligation upon young dons to support the newly refurbished Festival Theatre active under the guidance of Terence Gray and soon to become nursery to such admirable artists as Flora Robson and Robert Donat. Our weekly booking yielded us a crop of programmes conspicuous by their inverted chiaroscuro printing for consultation in the darkened theatre: these later achieved some collecting rarity and I remember that we sold our own set for half-a-crown apiece. A gentle and distinctly Clare flavour attends recollection of one particular visit to the Festival Theatre to which we had invited Will Telfer, Dean of Clare. We left after the performance and retrieved the 'Baby Austin'

South face of Finella after redecoration in 1929

in which we had arrived and which had been newly serviced by the local garage. We could count on Telfer not to feel superior to our transport and he swiftly tucked himself into the front passenger seat as we set off down the slope of Maid's Causeway, the street lamps illuminating the departing theatre crowds and streams of taxis arriving to meet their passengers. To my horror, events now portended disaster: slowly the front left side of the car tipped downwards (balanced in part by Margaret in the right rear seat), and I was hypnotised by sight of the nearside wheel trundling down the asphalt ahead of us and gaining ground, a spectacle not missed by returning undergraduates who happily cheered the contestants from the sidewalk. The confounded garage mechanics had, it was evident, replaced the four wheels after interchanging them, but had omitted the formality of securing any of the locking nuts. Need one add, the car tipped down upon the brake-drum and I tried to calculate how best one should use, or not use, the brakes to halt our progress as we swung left and right through the ranks of approaching taxi-cabs. Mercifully halted under the causeway trees, Telfer without a word opened his side door and sped off into the night. This was by no means the reaction of fear but shewed the experienced college officer instantly appreciating that at all costs the errant wheel had to be rescued from the cheering students who might at any moment fancy it as a trophy for college rooms: indeed Telfer, long a supporter of the University Hare and Hounds, reappeared in our head-lights with wheel beneath his arm, and behind him a helpful retinue of members of the Clare boat club like ourselves finishing the theatre performance in style. They lent powerful shoulders to lift up the car front, confirmed the replaced wheel locking it securely and waved us off back to college.

When, during the Second World War, Telfer had become the Ely Professor of Divinity, he regularly accepted as part of the air-raid duty, his midnight patrols of the exposed high cat-walks over the roofs of the vast cathedral. How distant from my own

Finella: the hallway redesigned by Raymond McGrath and Manny with
profuse use of glass and reflected light on walls and ceilings

conception of a pleasant stroll and how easy by contrast the walk-ways of the Clare buildings that were my route.

By the middle of 1928 we had undertaken to share with Manny Forbes the tenancy of his projected new home on the Backs, the house later christened 'Finella', but a year of very uncomfortable temporary shifts of lodging intervened before we took up residence there in the late summer of 1929.

Finella owed its origin in its realisable form to the purely chance encounter in an eating house near the National Gallery of Manny with an architectural student, Raymond McGrath, who had qualified in the highly regarded school of architecture in Sydney and was now seeking wider European experience. Immediately responsive to one another, it proved relatively easy to persuade the young Australian to change course and take up residence in Cambridge as a member of Clare. Manny could not have found a more sensitive or more compatible assistant in his design of converting the Victorian mansion, leased from Caius College, into an elegant modern house displaying all the visual qualities of modern decoration and furnishing.

It is part of the social history of Cambridge that the experiment was intensely successful, a success happily documented in the architectural journals, and testified to by the floods of visitors who struggled through our rooms at any hour of the day or night: in the first year three thousand signed the visitors' book, but we reckoned that barely one in four of the gazers had bothered with this formality, and certainly one had to lock the door before bathing lest one should be also on view, even in the small hours of the morning. This publicity Manny rightly welcomed as evidence of interest in and even of attraction to an appreciation of visual aesthetics, and he brought the excitement to a crescendo in the summer of 1930 by arranging that Epstein's massive and controversial statue 'Genesis' should be on display in the house during May Week. I remember that the palaver of guarding the work against possible vandalism from the unpersuaded, and the complexities of paying entertainment' tax on the admission charge, made for much confusion in the household, but in the end 'Genesis' was peacefully returned to Manchester. With his strong sympathy for imaginative schemes of social betterment it was inevitable that Manny should be drawn into a continuing admiration and varying friendship with Henry Morris, the forceful director of education for the county and creator first of the concept, and later of the reality of the Village College scheme. This unquestionably was an educational innovation of the highest significance, acknowledged as such both nationally and internationally. This success put upon Morris the entertainment of a continuous flow of visitors, a large proportion of whom he escorted, in the early 1930s, in visits to Finella. Manny's warm generosity was freely extended to these unannounced visitors and Morris had no scruples about deflecting to them refreshments laid on for Manny's own guests. We were ourselves living in Finella at this time and had every opportunity of realising that as between Manny and Henry Morris, Manny was much the more sympathetic and generous. This realisation gave particular appropriateness to the account, largely derived first-hand from Manny, of the episode that first split their friendship.

Henry Morris at this time had a flat on the first floor of the handsome Georgian bookshop of Galloway and Porter half-way along Trinity Street, and he furnished and kept it meticulously. To this locus in the small hours of Burns' Night came Mansfield Forbes, tired after foursome reels in the Market Place but sustained with only liquid refreshment permissible on this occasion, Drambuie and Scotch itself. By now, as Manny afterwards explained, it had become crystal clear to him that this intake was about to initiate a night of unspeakable stomach disorder, certified by the fact that he had no remaining stock of the tried antacidic remedy, Dr Jenner's Absorbent Lozenges, as especially recommended to pregnant mothers-to-be, but an infallible specific also for Manny's own digestive troubles. As the horror of this situation ripened, Manny realised that

'Enter these enchanted woods, you who dare': Raymond McGrath's
wood-engraving in illustration of a poem by G. Meredith

salvation lay at hand, for there was still a light in Henry
Morris's window and had he not himself recommended the
life-saving tablets to Henry? Summons by voice, and optimistic
knocks on the street door eliciting no response, Manny, stoked
by internal fires, sought other means of attracting attention. He
found these in the dustbins set out for clearance on the
pavement fronting Matthew's Café, and choosing a suitable tin,
empty of its canned fruit, he stood on the pavement and gently
lobbed it up at Henry's window. At first out of range, finally
one throw, horror of horrors, smashed the ancient window: the
light was sharply put out and no further sign of the tenant
emerged.

Manny took himself home, fury at this betrayal by his
potential rescuer adding ferment to his correctly anticipated

agonies. Next day Henry Morris, dignity mightily affronted by the midnight display of low rowdyism, visited Finella to explain in language derived extensively from Freud the extent of his affront. I gather Manny's hurt feelings caused similar responses and henceforth relations had a changed footing.

Manny's consuming interests in the whole field of visual aesthetics extended to a wide public in the days of Finella but were apparent through all the time I knew him. When I had first been elected a fellow he had at once sought my help in the recreation of the college 'Dilettanti' society. It was a club mainly of undergraduates, united by enthusiastic curiosity about art, literature and philosophy, drawn without distinction of subjects being read or prowess in other circles, but united by a considerable tolerance, wit and good humour, and a penchant for vigorous discussion and dinners of a somewhat 'mardi gras' character. The venture proved reasonably successful, naturally deriving its vitality in great part from Manny himself, although it was no exception to the rule that such societies rise and fall and will not be compelled if the magic mood is absent.

Lively accounts of the meetings of the 'Dilly' appeared each term in the *Lady Clare Magazine* whose editors were in large part adherents of Manny. The pages now displayed beautiful wood-cut illustrations by McGrath, who had remarkable command of this medium, and by others whom he instructed and encouraged. Among these C. F. Millett designed a series of black and white cartoon headings for the club reports, so vigorous, witty and instantly evocative that they have continued in use long after the artist's name has been forgotten. A source of more than competent poetry was headed by A. C. Frost. My own cover design, a picture of the college bridge heavily cut on the plank of a wood-block, was superseded by a characteristic McGrath design of skill and grace.

It was not surprising that the *Lady Clare* had now become outstanding among college magazines or that enthusiasm for its production should finally have outrun discretion.

During 1932 the editorship had somehow involved Manny

in an attempt to make the current issue a monumental one. This resulted in a very handsome but very large number that was printed off without much consideration of the ultimate funding, which was the responsibility of the Amalgamated Clubs. An early copy coming into the hands of the Master, he was deeply affronted, not only by the irregular over-expansion but by a skilful and barbed poem entitled 'Colonels' that he took, with some reason, to be aimed at himself. The issue was suspended and a college meeting called for consideration of the matter. Nothing but withdrawal of the offending publication would satisfy Wilson, and (as was apt to follow in these explosive situations), Telfer and I were instructed to cooperate with Manny in devising from the corpse a slenderer and purer version, whilst oblivion waited upon the offending issue. It was a pity in many ways, for several notable college achievements were recorded with wit and vivacity in the lost pages. Happily the junior *ersatz* editor retained enough to allow quotation of a section of the offending poem.

COLONELS

"Who stand at the gates of their pined villas at evening,
The Colonels, the backsides of Empire, once kicked, now
    happily kicking,
Who stand at the gates, in mufti, filling pipes in shirt sleeves,
Who in the Bordon twilight meditatively stand –
Do they contemplate the inside of the universe?
Or the still sad music of humanity?
Or do they, blank, misgive?"

"Who so arrogant to deny the Wordsworthian perceptions
Of Colonels, standing in the Blackdown twilight,
Gazing across the valley of Chamonix
At the prammed heir of the Jones's?"

"Who will deny the intimations of immortality of those
Who utter crisp commands to wife, and beat
For the ultimate straightening of their spines, their children;

Who have solved the problem of the universe and proved
The insanity of pacifists: the ultimate depravity of Art;
Who have sat in Judgment on the subaltern who married an
    actress;
Who know that only War is a better school than Wellington;
Who, being now retired, go with their pension to the saloon bar,
    the long lost uncles of bar-maids;
Who, trotting up to lecterns, mouth the words of Isaiah;"

and so on to a gentle ending

"They remember Poona, and the laughter of halfe-caste girls."

One may guess that fifty years on, *lèse-majesté* would not have called for such a public admission that the billet had indeed been so painfully, if glancingly hit.

Upon the constant excitements of the evolution and exposition of Finella during 1929 and 1930 were superposed, for Margaret and myself, the almost overwhelming preoccupations of the Fifth International Botanical Congress, the largest and most prestigious of gatherings of botanical scientists, now meeting for the first time in Britain under the Presidency of Professor A. C. Seward and centred primarily in Cambridge. The event brought a flood of organisational and executive work upon the staff of the Botany School and especially upon F. T. Brooks, the Cambridge Secretary. A. G. Tansley was largely responsible for the ecological section of which I was made co-secretary. Now, for the first time I was able to meet personally most of those eminent pioneers of plant-ecology whose work and reputation were hitherto known to me only in print. In fact it proved possible to conduct a large group of them over my own research territory at Wicken Fen. Margaret took responsibility for booking and accounting for all the numerous excursions and travel arrangements, no light task in a conference attended by over 1,000, most of them foreign and deeply mistrustful of the non-metric British coinage, so that each evening she returned to the bank a substantial weight of half-crowns that no visitor really trusted to out-value the comprehensible florin.

In the summer of 1930 congestion was heightened further for us by two factors. We had to accommodate for the meeting a young Swedish ecologist, Bertil Lindquist, who was to address the Congress upon the beech forests of southern Sweden. Poor man, he got very scant attention from us, but in later years he became a close friend with whom we stayed in Gothenburg, where he had become Director of the notable Botanic Garden in that city. As if this were not enough distraction, this was also the time we had been forced to choose for commencing the vacation of Finella in favour of a house of our own, a delightful old property 'Frostlake Cottage' in Malting Lane, between the Newnham mill-pool and the main entrance to Newnham. We were saved only by the devotion of Mr and Mrs George Roberts who had previously been my gyp and bedmaker. He had all the practical experience of the son of a working builder and together they now set us free from anxiety about making our new home fit for occupation.

Manny died in 1936 of a coronary embolism, and now Finella took on a legendary status like the Scottish queen after whom she had been named. It was found that Manny had bequeathed his extensive book collection, including first editions 'laid down like port' to be the basis for the College's student library. Despite the affair of the defoliation of the Dictionary of National Biography, Manny's generosity had been quite unimpaired and many of us recalled how, when he purchased a new book necessary for reading by his 'English' students, he would buy several copies at once and walk round when rooms were likely to be vacated, to leave a copy 'for free' on the table of a poorer student, likely otherwise to go without. At the sale of his effects I managed to buy a painting by Ethelbert White of which he had been fond, of the 'Old Bridge at Toledo'. It was intended as a *Denkmal* for the 'Forbes Library' and a look at the list of subscribers attached to the back of it conveys a reminder of the quality of those who esteemed Manny as a friend: they are a small sample of a very large population.

XII

HENRY

ADJACENT to Manny Forbes on the corner staircase, F, of the Old Court were the rooms of the Senior Tutor, Henry Thirkill, who from 1920 when he first assumed that office, to his death in 1971, played a role of overwhelming importance in the evolution of Clare. He was a great and modest man whose whole life was inspired by affection for the college and those many generations of its inhabitants with whom he dealt. The kindness he shewed me from undergraduate days extended to Margaret and our son David, in all through fifty years, and 'Uncle Henry' always accompanied the Godwin family on its summer holiday, an occasion to which he contributed a relaxed gaiety less evident on, shall we say, a meeting of the General Board. Even so he could not be far separated from his college and university preoccupations. He took along a dog-eared index of Clare men, and daily received from the college porter some forty or more letters that were expeditiously replied to by hand and duly posted in the course of a subsequent stroll. I recall well Henry's preoccupation with what the university would be best advised to do to replace J. T. Saunders as Secretary General of the Faculties upon his near retirement. After some three days of abstraction from the charms of the Walberswick scenery, the ejaculated 'Harry, I think I've got it' announced the solution, at once agreed by the university and admirable in operation, of transferring to this crucial post the then University Treasurer, H. M. Taylor. How many of our representatives, I wondered, brought such sustained deliberation to the university's management. These combined holidays highlighted for us the characteristic so well-known in Clare, of Henry's almost royal instant recollection of his former students, their families, careers and interests. One day as we were walking down Dawson Street in Dublin I drew Henry's attention to a man across the road and exclaimed that here was a man with a Clare tie. Henry spun round, crossed over and brought to us a man whose name he knew, and whose family he remembered in detail: despite the lapse of years, contact had been kept and was extensive and accurate. This kind of event sprinkled each holiday and at the small country hotel at Kilorglin in Kerry, it soon was evident that Henry's conversation with guests already there had disclosed links of more than the half of them with Clare and Clare men. It needs no elaboration from me to establish the fact that this wonderful quality rested upon Henry's intense interest in people and real concern for their welfare. In this attribute Margaret and he were excellently well matched, for, during the many years during which she was Secretary of the Cambridge Women's Welfare Association, my wife who did the personal interviewing of all the patients, had developed so sympathetic (and genuine) expression of attention and concern that she regularly attracted confidences even from total strangers encountered at hazard in a Sainsbury's queue, railway carriage or 'bus stop. Henry openly made enquiries of new acquaintances, but Margaret had no need for this: the two of them at the day's end knew all that signified of the lives and contacts of the hotel residents, though both were in fact extremely discreet. David and I merely accepted this virtuosity as totally out of our own reach.

It is difficult to think of any occupation or career in which Henry's fondness for people could have been more usefully employed than that of Tutor, and subsequenly Master of a college. It was by no means that he could not have established for himself a distinguished academic career. He had already in 1912 been appointed to the staff of the Cavendish Laboratory under J. J. Thomson and the research done thereafter and published in *Proceedings of the Royal Society* still retains its authority. He continued to lecture in physics until 1933, but although he had effectively closed his scientific career when he took over the tutorship, he kept a close friendship with former colleagues at the Cavendish and when we lived in Finella we saw that our neighbour, Lord Rutherford, was one of Henry's regular companions in afternoon walks.

It was hard to realise how far his modesty cloaked Henry's ability, and unwary university thrusters too often discounted him. It is *à propos* to recall how Brian Pippard brought to dinner in Clare, during Henry's mastership, that pre-eminent physicist, Heisenberg. They conversed amicably in the Combination Room and Heisenberg later confided that he had begun by regarding the Master as a conventional lightweight, until it was suddenly borne in upon him that the course of the conversation had been entirely controlled and his own attitudes quietly elicited by his seemingly ineffective host. The success of Henry's approach depended of course upon the serious reality of his concern for people, a concern extending through from the college servants and undergraduates to recipients of the university's highest honours.

When we were undergraduates some of us sought to sustain our studies by a promise to continue work in the evening until Henry's light was put out. Alas for good intentions, by two or three a.m. we gave up the competition with the Tutor, still working hard and efficiently, very often upon the dreary task of correcting school examination scripts so that he might have money to lend to impoverished students. It much suited his temperament to entertain, and his breakfast and dinner parties were frequent and jovial, illuminated by the evident pleasure Henry took in lavishing food and drink upon us all. It has been written by a former student that to 'Thirks' all the undergraduates were 'men', uniformly 'treated with politeness, gentleness and respect', their troubles and problems nevertheless shouldered whenever need arose. When Henry died, among his effects was an album composed for him by his men, to illustrate how they had occupied themselves during their absence from the university in the General Strike of 1926. This was placed in the college archives, a remarkably direct and faithful fragment of social history and a reflection of the admirable closeness of the Tutor's relation to his students.

As a boy in Bradford Henry was a keen supporter of the Yorkshire cricket team and would walk considerable distances to see his heroes: he was in fact a respectable spin-bowler himself and a useful member of Long Vacation cricket sides. In

College servants at bowls. The Senior Tutor, Henry Thirkill and George A. Roberts, trustiest of college servants

this as in other sports he readily shared undergraduate enthusiasms. He was a good pianist and found it easy to foster musical interests from the big drawing room on F staircase. The further, and invaluable tutorial attribute was a very considerable sense of humour, deliberately provoked in the Combination Room by Manny and Raymond Priestley, and easily induced by David's childish antics when we were on holiday together. It needed the relaxation of the Long Vacation and a half-empty college to evoke an unsuspected talent for practical joking. Four or five of us remained after coffee on a warm sunny evening in a Combination Room with sash windows open. We retired leaving Darby Nock, but no sooner were we gone that he leapt to his feet, and through the window asked Henry to throw up the Combination Room key. The first throw was short, but the next rose in a gentle arc through the open window and gently fell some six inches upon Nock's well covered pate. After a slight yelp the key was retrieved, thanks duly made and we went our several ways. Only next day did Henry report his prank. Not long after our departure the hypochondriacal Nock had reflected upon the possible damage inflicted on his skull by the falling key. Though exploratory fingers failed to find blood, he was impelled to seek advice and comfort from the Tutor. Henry, tickled by the absurdity of the request and undeniably naughty, sat Nock at the dressing-table in the bedroom, procured an electric torch, scissors and iodine and proceeded to a mock investigation of the cranium during which an increasing area was denuded of its hair. Henry found it impossible in the end to repress the giggles that the unfamiliar sight provoked, so that when he finally allowed the victim a hand-mirror the devastation was only too apparent. At last aware that he was subject to a mere practical joke, the incensed Nock exclaimed that he now would be forced to have a hair-cut, and blamed Henry, reasonably enough for everything. Poor Nock, the antics of the Clare community were proving too robust for him, and maybe this episode had some part in his decision later on to accept a chair in Harvard. Perhaps it was as well that Henry's aptitudes in this direction were so seldom displayed.

The Tutor in Clare after the First World War was entirely responsible for admissions and part of the policy for which he was responsible involved the group of colleges with whom we combined for the Entrance Scholarship Examinations. The groups in these years were often rearranged, but on Henry's advice we adhered to that which included Trinity, often taking advantage of second choices of able men excluded from their primary choice in Trinity by the local competition, and in any event allowing our examiners a look at what possibly was the strongest part of the Cambridge entry. For many years I was secretary of the science examiners in the Trinity group and had the pleasure each December of witnessing the great J. J. Thomson at work as chairman, sifting the results swiftly and accurately, never missing a top-notch Trinity candidate, and, with a fearsome clash of false teeth conceding now and then the claims of some other college to a man of good performance, and the quite audible aside 'Must leave something for the sharks, I suppose'.

The recruitment of able students owed something to this painstaking exercise in which so many of us participated, but much more derived from Henry's own percipience and the assiduity with which he established an empire of friendship and trust with the housemasters of the good public schools of the country and many also of the private day schools.' His correspondents were aware of those qualities of leadership, judgment and responsibility that Clare, through its Tutor, set store upon: they trustfully recommended such young men to the college knowing how carefully they would be cherished, often to exercise important office not only in Clare, but afterwards in the running of business and government of the country. It surprised us not at all to hear Henry referred to in school circles as 'the best tutor in either University,' nor, when he later came to hold the higher offices of the craft of

Freemasonry did he lack friends over the whole country and outside close academic circles.

Henry's own judgment was never better seen than in his admission of E. C. Bullard, the eminent geophysicist, as commoner in Clare after he had been turned down a year previously (admittedly after deficient schooling) by another college. Henry could not resist a smile of gratification as he told me that 'Teddy' had been admitted a fellow of the Royal Society almost indecently soon, when indeed he was aged twenty-six! I feel sure that Henry never bragged to the college that failed to make the prior catch, but this was not so with all cases of inter-collegiate competition for men. Before Henry's day Clare had turned off a student member whose scholastic performance seemed inadequate, but who then successfully sought admission in Downing College where there evidently were vacancies. In the course of years this man, now Master of Arts, in very proper gratitude left to his new college a handsome endowment employed for new building in the Court. It was my happy good fortune to be with Henry and Sir Lionel Whitby, both agreeably robed, one day when together they passed along the frontage of the Downing College Chapel building. Turning to the Master of Clare, the Master of Downing swept off his mortarboard gracefully and declaimed for Henry's benefit 'In piam memoriam, Magister Greystone'. A palpable hit, indeed!

The number of fellows in Clare between the two wars was small and several were preoccupied with important university posts, one or two were too ancient or too juvenile for central college authority, so that in effect the whole-time college officers amounted only to the Senior Tutor (Henry Thirkill), the Bursar, (until 1929 G. H. A. Wilson and thereafter W. J. Harrison) and Will Telfer as Dean and Assistant Tutor. It followed from both the nature of the post and the character of the man that the leadership in this triumvirate, financial matters apart, should naturally fall to the Tutor, whose office naturally required him constantly to plan and forecast the directions in which college policy should aim. It was always Henry's habit

'Henry' – Sir Henry Thirkill, C.B.E., M.C., Master 1939–59

to prepare fully beforehand, and he would consult all fellows
liable to be concerned with topics under consideration so that
he appeared at the meetings rather to act as a coordinator of
the fellows' wishes than as an originator of policy. The
smoothness and effectiveness of the meetings of Governing Body
and Council were phenomenal, and when the mastership was

vacated in 1939 by Wilson's retirement, the election of Henry Thirkill was instant and unopposed. In later years as the college body enlarged and more 'activist' attitudes became evident throughout universities, to some extent there was a tendency to see the smooth operation of affairs as the result of 'paternalism' and 'fixing' beforehand. Such feelings were perhaps most apparent when the time finally arrived to elect a successor to Henry in the mastership, and the fellowship abandoned its former policy of selecting within the ranks of its own members or graduates of Oxford and Cambridge.

The interest in all manner of visual aesthetics that so preoccupied the life of Mansfield Forbes was quite absent from the make-up of his close friend, Henry Thirkill. This came most strongly to my notice when it was arranged in the later years of Henry's mastership, that the college should have his portrait painted. The outcome was an excellent painting by Wilfred de Glehn, R.A., who employed the difficult but effective back-lighting of a seat by the north-west window of the Combination Room to establish the commanding proportions of Henry's head. The portrait, well-received at first, shewed the Master with a serious and thoughtful expression familiar to him when controlling college or university business, and entirely characteristic of the man. As more and more old Clare men viewed the portrait, it was evident that they saw in it nothing of the kindly father-figure and jovial host of their student days, who had entertained and guided them so effectively. They were disapproving and in time Henry also 'took against it', and thereafter made do with an *ersatz* painting that looked what it was, a competent derivative of a happily posed photograph with the desired expression.

This episode of course was many years after Manny's death, but it recalled inevitably to me Manny's part in a similar episode arising from the commission by the college of a portrait of the ageing Master, W. L. Mollison. Here on Manny's fortunate recommendation Henry Lamb was employed, and produced a marvellously good picture, possibly the best of our portraits. It actively displeased the sitter however, and he was not assuaged by the explanation that the green tinge of his beard was due to light reflected from the lawn outside the Lodge window where he was painted. When, at Mollison's demise, the portrait was looked for it was run to earth behind a book-case, face to the wall! The hiatus that accompanied this discovery was only partly made good by a posthumous portrait of Mollison produced by Hugh Buss, an old Clare man resident in Cambridge who had exhibited in the Academy and had painted successful studies of the college combination rooms in both St John's and Clare. History has given a faintly odd twist to this progression by the fact that each fellow was permitted, under Mollison's will to choose some memento for himself and Manny took a picture from the corridor wall in the Lodge. He had noticed it long before and appraised it modestly as a competent small land/sea-scape of the chalk coast near Dieppe, clearly signed by Sickert père. It was lost sight of after Manny's death in 1936, but thereafter has reappeared at intervals at property sales in Cambridge, where doubtless an enthusiastic purchaser glancing at the signature assured himself that this could indeed be by the esteemed Walter Sickert. The real painter identified, or the owner now beyond caring, the painting headed for another sale. It was better enjoyed for its own sake!

By the late 1940s the college had recovered substantially from the disturbances of the War and the decision had been taken to erect, as a memorial to those killed in the War, a new court extending southwards from the existing building. The Master had written personally to explain our intentions to every old Clare man whose address was known, and King's College had most generously agreed to let us have the proximal edge of their Fellows' Garden where it was needed to provide adequate breadth to the projected court, for which plans had been prepared by Sir Giles Gilbert Scott. Now that the plans were approved, the college had the happy thought to record its indebtedness to the trio of its officers whose devotion and skill

Combination Room consultation by college officers in Clare. H. Thirkill (Master), W. Telfer (Dean) and W. J. Harrison (Bursar)

had concentrated upon making this possible, and the painting of a conversation-piece shewing the three of them was commissioned. Terence Cuneo's painting shews Henry Thirkill, (Master), W. Telfer (Dean) and W. J. Harrison (Bursar) at the close of an informal committee in the Combination Room, where behind them through the window one sees the east range of the Old Court overtopped by the pinnacles of King's College Chapel. Very few examples of the 'conversation piece' genre exist in Cambridge colleges and it is pleasant that this example has achieved such a felicitous comment on the character of the men depicted and the times they served.

The new Memorial building was soon christened 'Thirkill Court' and was graced by the Henry Moore bronze of a falling warrior, movingly appropriate to this setting and evidence of a welcome move by the college to experiment with the introduction of modern sculpture in its courts and green spaces. It is an intention of which Manny would have approved.

XIII
'A. G'

My interest in ecology, evident already at school, although originating in causes I have never been able to identify, was maintained in undergraduate days. Mr A. G. Tansley returning to the Botany School from his war-time post in London, gave lectures for both parts of the Tripos, and before long an active 'Ecology Club' was informally established in the department. Of this I found myself, before long, the secretary. Under its auspices a party led by Tansley and S. M. Wadham, then Senior Demonstrator, bicycled out by way of Waterbeach and the 'Five miles from Anywhere' ferry at Upware to inspect Wicken Fen. This 1921 visit was my first introduction to the wonderful reserve of fenland that was to be the centre of my field studies in plant ecology over a great many years to follow.

Sam Wadham, whose assistant demonstrator I became, confided in me his opinion that at this time Tansley's advanced lectures were the best given in the department, no mean claim in a school where both A. C. Seward and F. F. Blackman also regularly taught. It was Tansley's clear logic, lucid exposition and fearless enthusiasm for a new field of science that commanded so much respect, particularly from the many senior students and visiting research workers drawn to them. In these early days, although I saw rather little of him, Tansley was very helpful in discussion of ecological problems and helped me directly in initiating field records and experimentation at Wicken Fen. These activities accompanied my main line of plant physiological research and for at least one day in the week allowed me to exchange the confines of the laboratory for the open air and direct contact with the world of free living plants.

In 1923 I began the recording of vegetational composition

'A. G.' Sir Arthur Tansley, F.R.S., Sherardian Professor of Botany in Oxford; world leader in fields of ecology and conservation

in exactly marked localities in the fen to determine the reality and processes of progressive changes at work there, either natural or determined by the regime of cutting of crops of the giant sedge for thatch and kindling, or of more palatable sedge and grasses for litter and coarse hay. In other reserved areas the growth was charted of the shrubs that invaded the uncut sedge vegetation: one such area, initally surveyed in 1923/25 was most recently remapped in 1972. The result of these combined observations was the recognition of the natural succession of fen vegetation through progressive growth of peat formed from water-logged plant detritus, but of more consequence was the recognition that under maintained crop-taking the same influences would operate, but be modified to give fresh vegetation types capable of withstanding cutting at yearly or longer intervals. The *natural* succession was thus *deflected* but not arrested. Tansley, in taking over this concept

147

identified such sequences as *plagioseres*, i.e., deflections from the natural development from water-logged grounds to fen, the normal *hydrosere*. In pursuit of the agency inducing the progression of the hydrosere I now undertook various studies of the water-level relationships on the fen, in part with my first research student, F. H. Bharucha.

The various subjects of these researchers were described in a sequence of papers published in the *Journal of Ecology* between 1929 and 1943. In preparing these I had the great advantage of Tansley's superb qualities as editor: he took endless trouble and had the knack of suggesting changes of wording that immediately illuminated one's own thoughts. He was deeply interested in the ecology of Wicken Fen and he and I together wrote an account of the vegetation, as part of *The Natural History of Wicken Fen*. It was these contacts, no doubt, that led A. G.

Main Lode, Wicken Fen; The Sedge-Fen with bush-colonisation, the lode with Gault Clay outer bank and beyond it the lowered level of drained .fenland

to offer me invaluable help in establishing my career as ecologist and botanist.

Although I was too young to be aware of it, the period covering the First World War witnessed a strong movement by young and active botanists in this country to reform the whole area of botanical teaching and to make it conform to the rapid changes taking place in the whole field of biological and scientific thought. Tansley, as editor of the *New Phytologist* gave active support to the wide introduction of elements of genetics, plant physiology, biochemistry and ecology into university teaching, and wished courses to be more experimental and to have closer relation to applied biology in areas such as forestry and agriculture. It was an age of strong paternalistic control in university departments and firm, even acrid replies were publicly made to the arguments of the reformers, notably by

Landward termination of the Main Lode in the village lane at Wicken, where it delivers the crops of reed used for thatch

such as Professor Seward, who was himself an intensely successful and popular lecturer. Certainly the campaign yielded no quick success, and as much could be said for the subject of ecology, in which Tansley had now become an acknowledged leader. I myself was urged by more than one leading botanist in the middle 1920s, to give up my concern with ecology and in my own interest abandon an area which they were sure had no future. The times were especially hard for Tansley, firmly opposed in his own university department and committed by a disability to a routine clerking post in the war-machinery centred in London. It was during this time that he took up his study of the works of Sigmund Freud which he was able to read in the German language. The upshot was so keen an interest that he wrote *The New Psychology and its relation to Life*, a book

Aquatic vegetation in the lode at Wicken Fen, with white water-lilies flowering above the deeper water and yellow lilies and bur-reed near the shallower margin

which after some trouble in securing an initial publisher, had a remarkable success and went into a long sequence of reprints and indeed translations. The large volume of public interest and requests for help that arose from the issue of this work persuaded Tansley that he should resign his university post and seek more direct instruction. Thus in 1923 he, with his wife and daughters went to live in Vienna, where he studied for several months under the guidance of Freud himself. Upon return to Cambridge he undertook the care of two or three psychological patients, but found conditions, including his own lack of medical training, to be inhibiting. Although now without a post, from his Grantchester home he continued to edit the *New Phytologist* and the *Journal of Ecology*, periodicals with whose foundation he had been very closely associated, and he wrote his *Text-book of Plant Biology* that described for the first time the integration of laboratory observations and experiments by students with the lecture courses themselves. Happily I was able to keep contact with A. G. and I was better able to entertain him now that I had a college fellowship. It was accordingly as a friend, if a very junior one, that in 1927 I was shewn an invitation to him to accept the Sherardian Chair of Botany at Oxford. I remember that A. G. replied to my warm recommendation to agree by saying that he had already sent an acceptance to the Vice-Chancellor. Our area of contact was widened by the fact that as undergraduate I had read those works of Freud available in English, and that for some time a close friend in Clare, E. G. Chambers, had attended the courses for Part II of the Tripos in Psychology (then part of the Moral Sciences Tripos), where he had exercised his facility for swift longhand recording of lectures. Thus in the late evenings the two of us had reconstructed, re-read and discussed the current views of such considerable scholars as W. H. R. Rivers. We not unnaturally had tried our hand at dream analysis and collected our own instances of the ' Psychopathology of everyday life'. I recollect that Tansley had come to have a very high regard for the scientific quality of Freud's mind and of the deep significance of his conclusions. He told me that during a three-parts serious Oxford social gathering, asked to name the person who, since the death of Christ, had most affected human thought and destiny, he had not hesitated to name Sigmund Freud or to defend his choice. As he took up the Oxford post A. G. resided during term in Magdalen College, but we saw him often at other times. When after the International Botanical Congress, we had gone in 1930 to live in Frostlake Cottage, Malting Lane, Margaret and he formed a very deep regard for one another and she shared with me strong admiration of his extremely liberal objectivity of mind and clarity of thought. There were no topics closed to discussion, nor could one employ the cliché or current prejudice without his revealing grin making one's failing clear.

Science without means of international communication is, in a family phrase, 'like a blind man made of smoke'. In this Seward and Tansley were agreed. Seward was Foreign Secretary of the Royal Society, and President of a great range of international scientific bodies, of which the Fifth International Botanical Congress had perhaps the greatest significance. Tansley to an even greater extent travelled abroad and like other great scholars, such as Joseph Needham, achieved higher reputation overseas than in his own country. This was what I soon recognised from the ecologists who came to the 1930 Congress, and equally during my visit to Rumania in the following year. By Tansley's recommendation I was attending the sixth meeting of the 'International Phytogeographic Excursion', a select international group whose meetings had been initiated by Tansley, who had personally brought together such a group in the British Isles during 1911. It was, just like the foundation of the *New Phytologist* in 1901, highly successful and another example of A. G.'s remarkable powers of timely innovation, in recognition of a scientific need. The guide that A. G. edited, and largely wrote, for the first meeting of the International Phytogeographic Excursion was an illustrated handbook *Types of British Vegetation* printed by the Cambridge

University Press and sold for six shillings. It was tremendously successful in its own right and came into such powerful demand that copies eventually fetched three pounds or more on the book-stalls. It was an important element in the rapid growth to acceptance of the whole concept of ecology, and it was with general approval that Tansley soon set about revising and re-issuing the work. He was indeed by far the most competent authority for such a task and when it appeared in 1939 it was a book of noble dimensions and great comprehensiveness. *The British Islands and their Vegetation* had emerged as a classic work of reference and scholarship.

As part of this displacement of A. G.'s activities, upon his removal to Oxford and after his organisational work for the Cambridge Congress had ended, he gave up the editorship of the journal he had founded in 1901, the *New Phytologist*. The ownership of the stock, the goodwill and a working capital of £100, were transferred to three young botanists, all lately working in Cambridge, A. R. Clapham, W. O. James and me. Although this was a substantial task it gave us great satisfaction and kept us very effectively in touch with the trends of botanical thought in the country, as well as, to some extent, overseas. Three decades later we in turn passed over ownership to another group of younger botanists who still carry forward its effective management. In 1932, shortly after taking up this editorship I was made Secretary of the British Ecological Society, a post so onerous that, but for Margaret's constant assistance, it would have been impossible. It involved at that time maintenance of a membership list of about 300, collection of membership fees and subscriptions, the regular holding of society and management committee meetings with preparation of accounts of all proceedings and the setting up of regular scientific meetings in London and provincial universities, to-gether with field meetings in the better weather for the demonstration of sites and areas where ecological work was active. We rapidly became personally known to most of the British membership, for attendances were very full, yielding satisfaction in the joint promotion of the new field of biological study, or perhaps one should write 'the new manner of approaching biology'.

During her first year in Cambridge Margaret, with Seward's readily granted permission, was able to attend most of the lectures and practical classes for Part II of the Tripos, finding them strikingly different from those she had taken in preparation for her London degree. She subsequently assisted the department in the semi-skilled labour of incorporation of additions to the Herbarium, and at the same time played a large part in

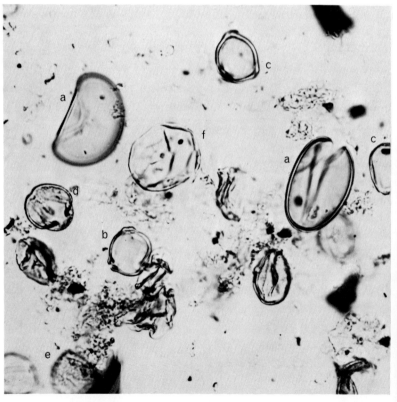

Microscopic residue of maceration of peat: the large bean-shaped objects are fern spores, most of the smaller are pollen-grains, many recognisable as birch, alder, oak etc.

illustrating and preparing for press the text-book *Plant Biology*, which I had written to correspond with the lectures I was giving to the first-year medical students. It was concerned with the principles underlying plant activity and structure and aimed to illustrate the general truths of biology, on which applied biology, such as medicine, agriculture or forestry, must eventually depend. The book, published in 1930, was readily accepted at both school and university level, and reappeared in four editions, the most recent in 1945.

The book finished, and preparations for the Botanical Congress well in hand, Margaret took occasion to seek A. G.'s advice as to a line of botanical research to which she might best direct herself. His reply turned out to be of the greatest consequence to our lives for he pointed at once to the recent publication by the Swede G. E. Erdtman of the methods and potentialities of microscopic identification of sub-fossil pollen-grains, recoverable in high frequency from recent geological deposits such as peat beds. The method had been worked out by the great leader of Swedish geology, Lennart von Post, although all accounts in English were due to his pupil, Erdtman. By statistical counts of tree-pollen at successive levels in undisturbed vertical series through a sediment, it was possible to reconstruct the major changes, through the period of deposition, in the forest vegetation dominant over most of western Europe since the ice-age. This technique, soon to be known as 'pollen-analysis' seemed to be a research tool of great power and promise: Margaret decided with alacrity to attempt its use. This seemed all the more appropriate since Cambridge sits on the edge of vast Fenland peat deposits, whilst I was already deep in consideration of the ecology of fen-vegetation, and the resources of the Botanic Garden and Botanical Herbarium were at hand to provide standard reference material. Erdtman had published in 1928 the gist of a swift reconnaisance of promising British areas, but vast territories of enquiry remained.

Professor Seward made available laboratory space and equipment including a good monocular microscope. Even the simplest preparations shewed our Fenland peats to be full of the pollen of our native flora, including an abundance of the tree genera. This pollen proved to be easily extracted from the peaty matrix and we could readily count the various types: we were launched now upon an enterprise that has not lost its impetus after fifty years, but which on the contrary has constantly widened its scope.

We were greatly favoured by the circumstances of time and place, for pollen-analysis proffered the means of meeting a need becoming sharply felt by archaeologists, geologists and many biological scientists, for a time-scale against which to set, and by which to compare, events of the most recent ten or twenty millennia, that is to say, since the close of the last Ice Age in Britain. So effective an introduction had been made in Scandinavia that we were rapidly presented with one opportunity after another of investigating promising sites to which it seemed that the technique might be applicable. Thus our field notebook for 11 March 1932 contains descriptions made when we examined the last stages of excavating the great King George V dock at Southampton where peat beds and tree layers alternated with estuarine clays and shell-marl to depths much below present sea-level. This visit, made at the suggestion of O. G. S. Crawford, was followed in April by one to Ingoldmells on the Lincolnshire coast, where we stayed at the sea-side home of that gifted geologist, Professor H. H. Swinnerton, whom we had both known in Nottingham and who had already thoroughly recorded the exposures of peat-beds on the changing foreshore. Here also we took careful series of samples. It was apparent that we were being swiftly drawn into studying those movements of land- and sea-level that are evident around our shores and Professor O. T. Jones invited us to look at a deep sequence of boxed samples taken for him at deep levels on the edge of Swansea Bay where the erection of a power station demanded geological information. On the eastern side of Britain again we went to inspect and sample deposits where the Middle Level outfall met excavations for a huge new sluice at St Germans.

Here in gum-boots and oilskins and with appropriate gear we recorded and sampled the successive peat and forest layers lying more than twenty feet below sea-level. A visit to Wicken Fen in September established that fen peat was continuous to a depth of at least twelve feet, and in December we have a record for borings at Plantation Farm, Shippea Hill, where the newly-formed Fenland Research Committee was beginning those investigations for which it was to become internationally famous.

Possibly the most sensational of the sites that we were engaged with was that of the Leman and Ower sandbanks off the Norfolk coast, where the skipper of the steam drifter, *Colinda* brought up from about twenty fathoms of water a lump of 'moorlog', the fresh-water peat here attached to the sea-floor. Breaking open a lump of this material he discovered a remarkable prehistoric implement, a notched bone point or fish-spear that was later recognised as similar to mesolithic artefacts known in Denmark and Estonia. He took the natural course of cleaning the implement and heaving the peat back overboard. He made good to some extent this loss of the opportunity of dating the bone tool by pollen-counting the embedding matrix, by going back and getting similar peat from the sea-bed. From this we made pollen-analyses that closely compared with similar samples sent to Erdtman: they related to a definite phase of West European forest history and strongly indicated that in mesolithic time the North Sea floor was still dry land passable on foot by prehistoric hunters.

As we pursued these early enquiries Margaret and I were training ourselves to recognise fossil pollen types in all attitudes and degrees of corrosion and we were improving and standardising the methods of preparation. Perhaps Erdtman was displeased that we had entered 'his' territory of the British Isles, for his replies to our approaches were not helpful and in effect we taught ourselves all the essentials of procedure. It will no doubt by now have become evident that what began solely as Margaret's research project, rapidly became a joint venture.

This was in part a consequence of the heavy pressure on my own time of lecturing, demonstrating and supervision, incidentally so irregular that the prolonged continuous laboratory attention demanded by experiments in plant physiology grew less and less attainable, and after scrapping several half-completed experiments at great waste of time and trouble, I recognised how much simpler I should find it to utilise broken time by sitting down to do microscopic counting of pollen. One must add of course that the elegance and promise of the pollen-analytic investigations drew me powerfully towards this opening field of 'palaeoecology'. Thus over the next few years there were compiled numerous papers under the authorship of 'H. and M. E. Godwin'. Not until domestic claims supervened did Margaret retire: it will suffice to say that I never have done so. The advice proffered by Tansley has indeed been among the most powerful directives shaping our lives: happily we shared his friendship and benefited from his counsel for many years.

XIV
EARLY DAYS IN THE LAB

THE BOTANY SCHOOL as I first knew it had been newly built for Marshall Ward but upon his premature death in 1906 it was taken over by Professor A. C. Seward. On the ground floor an excellent and capacious lecture theatre was flanked on one side by the herbarium, comprising a catacomb of cupboards housing a great reference collection of dried plants collected the world over. On the other flank was a museum full of interest to anyone like myself, avid to be acquainted with all sides of botany. Here were 'museum specimens' of algae, fungi, ferns, conifers and so on, cycad cones as big as your head, a sawn section of a giant red-wood, antarctic lichens from Mt Erebus and teaching exhibits harking back to Henslow and Darwin. There was also a thoroughly wide representation of exotic plant products shewing the origin and processing of the innumerable foods, textiles and building materials for which the world draws upon the plant kingdom. We now lose sight of the great significance of botanical science in discovering, transporting and establishing the vast empire of commerce and culture of plant materials, active in the great period of exploration and discovery that embraced the nineteenth century. I recall during a visit to Adelaide in 1965, seeing in the Botanic Garden a perfect vestigial specimen of a museum typical of those formerly devoted to celebrating and demonstrating the role of economic plants in the life of the world. This propaganda is now less strongly felt and in any event is undertaken by the new visual display media; it was only a few years before the Botany School museum was abandoned, the herbarium was transferred to the space thus freed and the former herbarium became an enlarged and highly efficient library. Whilst the museum still existed it was serviced by technicians who incorporated fresh specimens and kept up a regular battle with evaporation to ensure that

Sir Albert Seward, F.R.S., Professor of Botany in Cambridge, 1906–36. One time Master of Downing College, University Vice-Chancellor and holder of innumerable scientific distinctions, especially botanical and geological

the level of preservative in the hundreds of museum jars should not fall below danger line. In charge of this team was the senior assistant, most appropriately named Shrubbs, himself an old-fashioned botanist of great competence who, in his half-subterranean workshop made time to coach a certain number of undergraduates. I much respected his experience, especially after he discovered on his morning bicycle-ride to Cambridge from his home at Ickleton, a colony of the very rare lizard orchid flowering by the roadside, a treasure he took care to conserve from vandalism.

The changing emphasis in the world's appreciation of the role of the botanist in its economy was soon reflected by the new buildings added to the western end of the existing Botany School by the handsome benefaction of the Rockefeller Foundation. These housed the newly-created sub-departments of plant physiology and of mycology with plant pathology respectively under F. F. Blackman and F. T. Brooks: they signalled appreciation that these are sectors of science basic to agriculture. An equivalent provision of space was provided for teaching in a modern laboratory for some fifteen students for Part II of the Tripos, and Professor Seward's own palaeobotanical research was likewise catered for. It gave me a special satisfaction that Mr Blackman had made for the keystone of the doorway of the new extensions, a carving of the leaves of the maidenhair tree, *Ginkgo biloba*, male and female specimens of which have been grown as espaliers on the south face of the older block.

The 1906 Botany School itself had succeeded departmental buildings on a quite different site. Old engravings sometimes to be seen in the Cambridge print shops shew the pinnacles of King's College Chapel rising directly behind the glass-houses of the Botanic Garden. This, at first sight unlikely coincidence is explained by the circumstance that formerly the Botanic Garden was in the area between Downing Street, Free School Lane and Corn Exchange Street with the Department of Botany contiguous to it. In the 1920s the only visible evidence of this former siting was a great tree of *Sophora japonica* still magnificent in full flower. The Botanic Garden had been transferred to its present site in 1831, but the university now accepted the suggestion that a successor to the *Sophora* should be planted in the lawn before the present Botany School to preserve the long association. Happily the partnership persists.

Translocation was not the only change of note experienced by the Botanic Garden. In 1921, the year when I was taking Part II of the Tripos, the university for the first time appointed a Director to the Garden, a scientist with teaching duties in the Botanical Department and operating to maintain the necessary horticultural activities through an experienced superintendent. The new director was Humphrey Gilbert-Carter, a Cambridge graduate with an Edinburgh medical degree and considerable experience of Indian botany. He was to prove as puckish in the Botanical Department as 'Manny' Forbes in Clare, and had considerable facility in getting in the hair of Professors of Botany. He was none-the-less destined to exert a most profound influence on the shape of Cambridge botany, attracting the respect and affection of a notable school of younger taxonomists whose influence in constructing the new *Flora of the British Isles* and subsequently *Flora Europaea* was of outstanding scientific importance. 'Humphrey' taught taxonomy along his own highly idiosyncratic lines. He and his wife Doreen soon came to live in 'Cory Lodge', the colonial-style Director's residence built in the heart of the Garden, and thither each Sunday repaired a concourse of student friends, that gathered, two or more ranks deep, round the tea-table in a general atmosphere of joviality and chatter. Humphrey threw in medical school jocularity such as requesting the jam by 'please pass the goat's haemorrhage' or deposited Ben, the shaggy English sheep-dog, suddenly in the lap of any lady likely to be shocked.

He had a strong disposition to avoid giving anything resembling a formal lecture course, but relied upon the inspiration of the moment and spared no pains to carry interested students into the open countryside, where they fell into the trap laid by every real teacher, and began to think and work for themselves.

No doubt in part because it was *not* expected of him, he began early in his tenure to conduct regular classes in reading Virgil, a hint of his own tremendous affection for and skill with the mastery of languages both ancient and modern, asiatic as well as occidental. In later years he gave me ungrudging help in the translation of Scandinavian scientific publications and always assumed that I had been brought up on Grimm's Laws; I wished I had, but began to recognise them in time from Humphrey's well-worn mnemonics enshrining them.

In our Part II classes immediately after the first war we had the advantage of being taught also by another remarkable man, the botanist J. C. Willis, F.R.S., who had spent the greater part of his life in one or other of the great botanic gardens of the world and had recently retired from the directorship of that at Rio de Janeiro to seek a tax haven in the Channel Islands. He emerged during the Cambridge May Term to give lectures at Seward's invitation on plant geography and further to publicise his views at meetings of the learned scientific societies. He was a man with passion for and skill in the collection and analysis of data, by no means exclusively botanical. His *Dictionary of Flowering Plants and Ferns*, from its first edition in 1897, has not ceased to be a bible for generations of botanists, but he took time in passing to produce the successful *Tube-bus Guide to London*, published by C.U.P. in 1928. His many scientific papers culminated in the publication by the Cambridge Press in 1922 of his famous book, *Age and Area*, that takes its name from Willis's key biogeographic concept. The 1922 Part II botany class had a ring-side seat in the *Sturm und Drang* that publication of the book instantly attracted. It would be rash indeed of me to attempt any summary of Willis's views, but in effect he re-examined or greatly supplemented the data available on the distribution of plants (and to a lesser extent, animals) from the great days before conjectures arising from the naive early premises of the Natural Selection theory obfuscated the views of biologists. In the upshot he established that the evolution of new species on the one hand, and the natural spread of plants into undisturbed communities on the other, were both processes of similar pace, and were so slow that their consequences have been primary factors in shaping the present ranges of the existing flora of the world. Hence of course the species that had been longest in existence had come to occupy the widest territory; in fact this *was* 'Age and Area'.

Willis quoted to us from his vast experience instances, such as the spread of introduced foxglove, broom and bramble in New Zealand, of the rapid colonisation of exotic plants into landscape cleared of natural vegetation, and he contrasted this with the exceedingly slow penetration of introduced species of the Botanic Garden in Ceylon, into the untouched margin of the native woodland. He thus shewed us the strong influence of barriers to dispersal and referred back to his own student days when he and I. H. Burkill had shewn that in the fertile soil of the crowns of pollard willows in the valley of the Cam near Cambridge, not ten per cent of the plant species growing at ground-level were represented. The barrier of eight feet in height effectively prevented their migration.

This was a demonstration that appealed greatly to me and I looked around to see whether there were other instances at hand of barriers to dispersal affecting the range of the local flora. I soon found this to be supplied by a group of ponds dug in the gravels of the Trent Valley, between Nottingham and Derby. Vastly different in the content of aquatic flora, these ponds were shewn by historical records to be of various ages since the seventeenth century, and it was evident that they had all progressively suffered invasion by new species so that the oldest pond was richest. The differences between them were not due to local soil and water effects, but merely to chance in a process slowed by the necessity for the aquatics to surmount the land barriers.

It strikes me now that Seward may have been induced to invite Willis to assist the Tripos teaching by his own lasting concern with the problems of plant geography. However for my own part, not only were the observations on the Trent valley ponds the basis of my own first scientific paper (1923), but I found myself for a long time afterwards concerned with historical plant geography as it was increasingly affected by the factual evidence of the sub-fossil plant remains. In particular I was to find myself drawn into the controversy as to whether the British Isles had been swept clear of all plant life by the rigours of the latest Ice age and if so, by what means this *tabula rasa* had been recolonised. The evident role of the North Sea as a barrier to such reinvasion needs no emphasis, but it was not until Quaternary Research had advanced substantially that we were securely to document either survival of plants through the Ice Age in Britain or the progress of reinvasion from the continent.

I count myself most fortunate that in early student days I was exposed to the teaching ability and enthusiasm of such masters as Seward, Blackman and Tansley, all lecturers of the front rank. As it fell out my first-year practical classes in botany had to be taken in the afternoons when competition was light and I had a generous share of the demonstrator's attention, here provided by Dr Cyril West whose name was long associated with those of F. Kidd and G. E. Briggs in pioneer physiological studies of plant growth, but who proved himself in the years to come to be also an able taxonomist *manqué* and still, over the age of ninety, a devoted labourer in the Botany School herbarium. His conviction and skill would have convinced me, had I needed to be, of the supreme value to the biological student of examining fresh material for himself at every opportunity. In later years, when I was myself in charge of the elementary laboratory, no one more convincingly proved this than the formidable 'Becky' Saunders, who gathered all the Newnham and Girton students into her care and made certain that they saw for themselves every last bit of evidence the fresh material might yield: the rest of my demonstrators toiled far behind her in assiduity and skill. A very kind and competent Newnham don, she was an early President of the Genetical Society, and her upright carriage, masculine jacket and starched collar were liable to give rise to mistakes among pre-dinner guests catching sight of her across the Newnham College Hall. Of course, in field, laboratory and lecture-room alike it remains always the magic ability to convey enthusiasm on which one most relies, and I daresay my suggestibility played into many competent hands. There was a long period when I was very closely in touch with all the active young research students in the Botany School and used to exploit their kindness by getting them from time to time to demonstrate their experimental procedures to a small group of my college supervision students: these responded with the utmost enthusiasm to the glimpse of the gateways to botanical research, often learning much by questioning methods or argument at source.

In Cambridge, as in the country as a whole, during the opening decades of this century, botany was particularly well served by an abundance of able women scientists. They were recruited by the demand in girls' schools where botany was taught to satisfy the need now being accepted, to import science teaching into the curriculum: botany was less demanding of laboratory space and technical assistance than the physical sciences and more readily acceptable than zoology with its daunting dissections. None-the-less botanical study went a good way towards eliciting major biological principles, not least those of reproduction; gave familiarity with the techniques of comparative morphology and elementary physiology; and offered some familiarity with what is implied by adaptation and by evolution.

Encouraged by the heuristic methods introduced by T. H. Huxley in his own teaching, together with the stimulus of fresh biological discoveries, many able women pursued further botanical studies in the universities, the best of them becoming research workers of established reputation, as the scientific journals amply testify. I had myself been taught at school by a most able woman, Jennie Turner, and in my early years in Cambridge I was indebted not only to Miss Saunders, but also to two other outstanding women botanists.

The first of these was Mrs Agnes Arber, née Robertson, who

had been greatly encouraged in botanical studies by her great friend and teacher, Ethel Sargant. Agnes Robertson in 1909 had married the palaeobotanist E. Newell Arber and thereafter lived in Cambridge. She took little direct part in the work of college and university, but remained in closest touch with botanical thought, and pursued her work at home in a modest terrace house where she was always available to help colleagues. At Professor Seward's suggestion she made use of the fine collection in the Botany School Library to write her book on *Early printed Herbals*. Profusely illustrated and excellently produced by the Cambridge Press in 1912 it became a standard work that she largely rewrote for a revised edition in 1938. Equal success attended her later books on aquatic plants and upon two of the great divisions of the flowering plants. Her latest works turned to a consideration of scientific thought in relation to philosophy and metaphysics. Tansley wrote that 'Dr Agnes Arber is the most distinguished as well as the most erudite of British plant morphologists' and it was entirely appropriate not only that she received the Gold Medal of the Linnaean Society, but that she was the first woman botanist to be made a fellow of the Royal Society.

Students in the Botany School in the early post-war years were able to make easier contact with the second of the women botanists I mention, for Muriel Wheldale Onslow actually instructed our Part II Tripos class in practical plant-biochemistry, and we enjoyed the use of her 1920 book published by the University Press on that subject. She was apt to appear in a voluminous afternoon dress as if *en route* for a tea-engagement but the flounces and jewelry and pronouncedly feminine gestures did not lessen her competence in conducting the class or countering its crises. Her correct title was the Hon. Mrs Huia Onslow and she devoted herself unremittingly to pursuing with her husband the extensive genetical research that a climbing accident otherwise denied him. Like so many of the 'new' biologists in Cambridge they were deeply affected by the presence (though not in the Chair as many had hoped) of the

great pioneer geneticist, W. Bateson. In the house at Grantchester that bears still the plaque commemorating his residence
there, Bateson entertained his students and some, Mrs Onslow
among them were shewn the collection of post-impressionist
paintings that so delighted him, although over-risqué for
general display. After Margaret and I had been married and
I had the pleasure of doing some minor collaborative plant
physiology with Mrs Onslow, we would call upon her at her
flat in Clare Road. Here we were both stunned to see upon the
wall the picture once belonging to Bateson, of *Die Kranke
Prinzessin*. The pallid consumptive lady supported by anxious
attendants in the sombre yew-enclosed garden was by Edvard
Munch, and breathed unspeakable melancholy. Our hostess
then disclosed the story of how she had lost sight of the picture
after Bateson's death, and after a longish interval had sighted
it amongst the debris of a back-street junk shop in London,
whence in the end she had been able to retrieve it.

Practical plant physiology was under the direction of G. E.
Briggs who operated very disadvantageously from the outdated
manual by Darwin and Acton: he was so astringently critical
of the design of the experiments set for class exercises as to
involve all but a hardened few in feelings of severe inferiority.
All the same the survivors in the end came to respect and hope
to copy their mentor's severity of scientific procedure and
exactitude of argument. For F. F. Blackman, lecturing for both
parts of the Tripos was a process to which great care was
devoted and every one of the audience felt strongly at least the
illusion of comprehension. This level of scientific communication was admirable but it was, perhaps naturally, associated
with the most protracted and exacting gestation of the numerous
research projects developed by his research students. Although
their results were partially displayed in F. F.'s advanced lectures, publication in the scientific journals was held up by
constant revision and improvement, the work of one student
becoming log-jammed by the unpublished results of earlier
generations. One had to applaud the perfection of the ultimate

rare scientific publication by the master, but the consequences of this perfectionism bore hard upon young scientists overseas whose prospects of employment rested decisively upon the appearance of at least *some* published work. How often was I asked by such, 'when will Mr Blackman publish my results?' This was painfully unanswerable, as a stack of unpublished theses left upon Blackman's demise directly confirmed. Of course the habit of ultracareful preparation was in the interest of stemming the vice of compulsive instant publication, but here we felt the reticence was overdone, especially when we heard via sources outside Cambridge that a visiting American physiologist of some distinction, having read no paper by Blackman during the previous ten years assumed him to be dead and was staggered to be able to come to the Botany School to meet him. On hearing first-hand the great advances sponsored largely by Blackman, the visitor plaintively murmured that had he been told of this work his own research of the last decade might have been more usefully directed.

As I myself later on gathered experience, on the one hand as director of research students, as member of the Board of Research Studies and of various grant-awarding bodies, and on the other, as editor of papers submitted to different scientific journals, I became convinced of the great value of requiring every research student to submit a substantial *interim report* upon the results he had achieved and of the evidence on which they rested. I held strongly to the view, first of all, that such formulation of results is itself part of the exercise of research: it has been well said that results do not become science until they have been communicated and have thereby become common property, tested and relied upon by the scientific community. Moreover in the second place only by striving to express one's results and ideas with optimal clarity can a research worker, in many instances, himself become aware of the full implications of what he has achieved, or even those of the work on which he may still be engaged.

Many research students are very unskilled, and indeed

untrained in presenting scientific evidence and will handicap themselves unnecessarily for future publication as well as for presentation of a degree thesis if they neglect an early opportunity of practising the needful skill.

Finally, research supervisors for their own part can and should employ the preparation of the interim report on the one hand to train their student in scientific writing and (no less important) to inform themselves adequately of their student's real progress and potential for research. Only after this, it seems to me, can the supervisor effectively report to the departmental head or research foundation that supports the research project.

Although it might superficially seem a laborious exercise, the ultimate all-round saving of time and energy is enormous, not least in prospective editorial labour, and for the research student it seems appropriate to remind him that those who cannot stand the heat should stay out of the kitchen!

From the beginning research and teaching in the Botanical Department brought me more and more closely into familiarity with one of the most useful but unregarded tools of the scholar. This, the provision and circulation among research workers and science departments of cheap offprints of original publications, is a practice with which I had much to do, firstly as research student and director of research students, as librarian, departmental and university administrator, and not least as the editor of two journals, each supplying authors with reprints of their own publications at no more than a bare printing charge.

When research is active so that close and repeated consultation of the literature is needed, it is convenient neither to be tied to sojourning in libraries, nor to be taking home large bound volumes, or sneaking away still unbound parts of current issue, a practice rightly abhorred by good librarians. How much easier it is to consult a reprint of one's own, at once transportable and at hand. Thus for many years I regularly purchased 250 or 300 reprints of my own papers and circulated them to major departments and individuals actively concerned in the area of my own research. I bought the envelopes and provided postage, and in return received a steady flow of reciprocal offprints, thus keeping in fast and easy touch with recent findings in my own and related fields.

In later years the practice grew up among junior staff of expecting the departmental office to provide free envelopes and postage, whilst themselves retaining the return flow of reprints. This seemed to me an exploitation of university funds but it was not actively opposed. Indeed I once knew a very eminent professor who, upon retirement, actually *sold* to the university his collection of scientific reprints for the all-in price of one shilling a copy. It was deemed inexpedient to enquire who had paid for envelopes, addressing and postage of the outward flow of publications!

The incoming tide of paper took a good deal of housing: for my own part I solved the problem by getting a supply of suitable stiff cardboard boxes made to order in the Midlands, a source soon widely adopted by my colleagues. The Secretary-ship of the British Ecological Society and editorship of journals provided contacts that increased the range and volume of the inflow. Naturally by such a system one not only kept in touch with senior and established workers, but their younger associates took occasion to add their own names to the circulation lists. It was a singularly effective scientific information network that depended of course upon the willingness of editors of scientific journals to sustain the primary printing costs, giving contributors the advantage of reprints at a fraction of the real cost. Fundamental as this dependence is, it was surprisingly overlooked when, as I recount in Chapter xvii, the attempt was made to take over, for political reasons, control on a national scale of the publication and circulation of all scientific reprints.

I rapidly discovered the special advantages of reprint circulation that lie in subjects such as ecology and Quaternary Research, requiring as they do synthesis of information from the most diverse of sources. Results extend from fields of geography, geology, climatology and archaeology as well as the expected biological areas and results often appear in regional or even local societies seldom encountered in any specialised library and in few save the largest of extra-national ones. Thus, for example, a reprint from a Dane, describing his collaborative work with American excavators at an Iranian site, will by his offprint quickly inform a good proportion of his active overseas colleagues ignorant though they may be of the particular journal employed for publication.

In recent years, as costs of publication have multiplied, scientific journals have found themselves unable to go on subsidising cheap offprints: authors may indeed still buy them but only at prices vastly greater than formerly. Likewise postal rates have rocketed so that few young authors can afford more than a very restricted skeletal circulation. The action of journal proprietors in charging more highly was understandable and was accentuated by the goose-slaughtering practice begun by the heads of some scientific departments. These required their staff to purchase for them a supply of cheap reprints of all papers they might print in the year: these were now collected, roughly bound together and issued under the title of 'Annual Proceedings' of the department. In this manner the journals concerned at once were asked to bear all the costs and risks of editing, printing and publication whilst at the same time, the journal sales were being destroyed by the loss of customers, coming increasingly to rely upon such 'Annual Proceedings' circulated on an exchange basis between the issuing departments. A rise in reprint charges to a realistic level was a forseeable measure of self-defence that quickly followed.

The custom of active exchange of the scientific offprint within the circles of research workers formed the basis for the aggregation of great collections, more or less specialised in nature, that were filed or even bound together and that were often donated upon retirement or demise to centres of continuing growth. The Cambridge Botany School has had large acquisitions, amounting to thousands at a time, from the libraries of such pioneers as Sir Albert Seward and Sir Arthur Tansley, to expand its own considerable reprint collections.

Among the earliest and most famous of such reprint collections was that built up by Charles Darwin himself, presented to Cambridge University by his son, Sir Francis, Reader in Botany for many years. These papers, some of them annotated by Charles Darwin himself, remain in custody of the Professor of Botany, whoever he may chance to be. They were foresightedly listed in a printed catalogue put together by Sir Albert Seward, and among them was the bibliophilic prize, an original copy of *Das Kapital* inscribed by Karl Marx in presentation to Darwin: what a thrilling juxtaposition to rejoice the vision of Sir Geoffrey Keynes when he discovered it at large in a study drawer of Down House.

The diminution of interchange of scientific reprints between authors following upon increasing cost of the custom, has to some degree been counteracted by the increased use of microfilm and by the extended employment of mechanical duplicating machines. Some care however is needed in keeping clear of the copyright laws and neither technique offers the clarity, cheapness and convenience that formerly were associated with the employment of one's own offprint library. The growth, optimum and decline of the practice seem to warrant at least a footnote in the history of scientific ways and means.

XV
FENLAND STUDIES INTERRUPTED

ALREADY IN CHAPTER XIII I have given an indication of
how, in the early years of our marriage, Margaret and I came
to concentrate our research activities upon pollen-analysis and
its applications within that area of study since come to be known
as Quaternary Research i.e., that geological period embracing
the Ice Age and the time since then to the present day. The
Fenland Basin was not only conveniently adjacent but rich in
opportunities to recover evidence of past events such as
commanded the attention of zoologists, archaeologists, geographers and geologists both professional and amateur, who in
1932 came together as the Fenland Research Committee under
the chairmanship of Professor (later Sir) A. C. Seward. The
extremely acute and active secretary was Dr Grahame Clark,
later to be Professor of Archaeology and Master of Peterhouse,
and always at his shoulder the reassuring bulk of C. W. Phillips
and of Gordon Fowler, Transport Manager of the Ely Sugar
Beet Factory, both men of great resource and detailed familiarity
with the countryside. In appropriate groups we were summoned
to all promising sites with as little loss of time as possible, and
we dug, photographed, mapped and sampled to suit our
individual purposes, following up with laboratory and museum
investigation.

Considerably aided by the chronological scale provided by
our pollen-analyses, we were enabled to fit into one broad
sequential pattern the major features of evolution of the
Fenland, recognising the stages of infilling of the shallow basin
by alternate beds of brackish and fresh-water deposits, the latter
culminating in deep peat fens, bearing at their margins fen-
woods whose traces remain as buried forests, along with giant
bog-oaks of the former forest floor now water logged and buried

in peat. Former waterways were recognised in the 'roddons', low winding banks of silt meandering across the present-day black fens, and shell-marl deposits were identified as fresh-water meres adjacent to the roddons in their active phase. The contemporary fauna of the past was recovered and referred to the habitat of the time, as for example by whale vertebrae in the roddon silts, the giant aurochs from the buried high forest, and fossil foraminifera from the brackish-water Fen Clay. The deepest parts of the ancient rivers we were able to confirm as holding deposits from the transitional Late-glacial time, and on the banks of the streams there were recovered, stratified into the deposits, remains of successive human cultures. In particular in carefully organised deep excavations at Shippea Hill, the Fenland Research Committee proved no less than four distinct archaeological horizons, Mesolithic, Neolithic, Early Bronze Age and Roman.

There is no need here to pursue the detail of this effective collaboration since I was able afterwards to present it in the separate book *Fenland: its Ancient Past and Uncertain Future* in 1978. The results of our investigations were generally published in the specialist journals as soon as possible after conclusion, so that between 1933 and 1938 those most concerned were well aware of what was happening. In order however to reach the broad range of scientific and public interest it was arranged that, at the 1938 meeting of the British Association in Cambridge, I should give one of the prestigious 'Evening Addresses' upon the topical theme 'The History of the Fenland'. Sir Albert Seward, President-elect for the 1939 meeting, was fortunately at hand to facilitate practical arrangements to deliver the lecture in the newly opened Arts Theatre that held an audience far larger than any I had hitherto addressed and a theatre-manager notably convinced that we were likely at best to get a house quarter-full. The lecture was necessarily well illustrated by maps, pictures of sections, artefacts and so forth, but when on the preceding evening I went to try out the prepared lecture I made the horrible discovery that the slides regularly used in lecture-rooms with distances of about 50 feet or less to the screen, were totally unreadable in the theatre where the throw was 200 feet or more. I had no alternative but to rewrite my script, weeding out every slide with small lettering. Next morning I returned to the empty theatre only to find projection impossible from the usual operator's room, and we had to employ a fresh lantern perched upon the front of the dress circle. This provision meant such further sorting of illustrative pictures that there was no escape from rewriting a third version of the 'discourse', a task completed with little time in hand. I finally took the stage, fearing the very unfamiliar acoustics and dreading possible misrecollection of some main lead, entry or accent. To my immense relief the house was absolutely full and the audience entirely sympathetic to the romance of the Fenland story.

The British Association meeting for the following year was duly opened in Dundee on 30 August, by Sir Albert Seward, but after three days it was brought to a premature close by the onset of the Second World War. The active fellowship of scholars that constituted the Fenland Research Committee was now disbanded into a great variety of war occupations and never reassembled in its original form.

In the First World War it had been national policy to call up for National Service everyone reaching the age of eighteen, and to recruit officer ranks immediately from the school O.T.C.'s. Thus Oxford and Cambridge Colleges were thereby skeletonised, losing at once their whole undergraduate population and most of the teaching staff. It was quite different in the Second World War, during which the Government procedure maintained a substantial undergraduate population, securing the training of medical students, scientists and engineers before call-up, although residence was in most instances restricted to two years or somewhat less. Thus a proportion of more senior teachers, especially in the scientific disciplines, were retained at their posts although those of us so employed were naturally engaged on a plethora of war-time duties of every kind and the total staff of colleges and university shrank a good deal.

In the 'phoney-war' period the colleges displayed their inherent and traditional independence of mind. As they viewed the prospects of air-raids destroying their cherished buildings and homes, they (reasonably) judged it likely that in severe raids town water-supplies might fail: they therefore proceeded to equip themselves with portable fire-pumps that could draw water from the Cam or from static water-tanks. They were sardonic about the university administrators who declared that, since they paid town rates, they looked to the town to protect them!

The colleges set up a coordinating body to secure that they came to one another's help during air-attack. In Clare air-raid precautions occupied our thoughts a good deal and each Court had its own look-out posts, A.R.P. (Air Raid Precaution) centre and first-aid post. From the engine-house in the river-garden fellows, servants and undergraduates learned to run fire-hose to all parts of the Old Court and during the war period when he was in residence in Clare these teams were joined by the undergraduate King Peter of Jugoslavia.

It fell to me to act as secretary of the college A.R.P. groups and to establish liaison between them and the national organisation of the town. I recall the odd circumstance that when we were attending an instruction class upon possible hazards to be expected, we were lectured upon the fearful consequence of the use of Lewisite (mustard-gas). As the ghastly pictures of victims were circulated, the shining happy features were displayed of one man anxious to offer himself as 'guinea-pig' to the instructor so that the class could see the real thing: it was the clearest possible declaration of masochistic anticipation and was recognised at once and gently refused. An essential part of the liaison was the maintenance of a quick two-way traffic of information on the introduction of new types of offensive weapon and I spent much time soothing down hurt feelings when town A.R.P. officers learned of new weapons or procedures whilst their college colleagues were still uninformed. This was most sharply apparent on the day after our nearest 'incident' had damaged Whewell's Court, and allowed the Trinity A.R.P. officer, A. S. F. Gow, to identify and report to the authorities a type of German bomb not hitherto seen in this country. Unhappily, when details of the new weapon were circulated by the town service they failed to reach the colleges and Gow had the mortification of hearing therefore from outside, about his 'own' bomb. Gow was keen and choleric: he engaged me by telephone for over a half-hour and I counted it an achievement indeed when I had persuaded him not to refer the delinquent service to the highest government levels, as he was fully capable of doing. It was not until a fairly late stage in the War that the Government's introduction of a compulsory organisation of air-raid precautions obliged the university to appoint A.R.P. personnel and develop facilities to match and operate with those of the colleges.

From an early date about two-thirds of the Memorial Court was given over to the Royal Air Force Initial Training Wing and they were reinforced towards the end of the War by a small contingent of the Women's Auxiliary Air Force and of American Military Police. Happily not even this mixture proved to be explosive and this was a great boon to Professor Dixon Boyd and myself, for we jointly shared night-time responsibility for that court, sleeping in my room by the great gateway and just above the Porters' Lodge where we could directly hear the telephoned 'yellow' and 'red' alert messages by which the A.R.P. service was kept in touch with the onset and progress of raids. For a short uncomfortable period the Memorial Court was closed and fellows and students alike had to carry signed passes, but this phase passed with the diminishing apprehension of fifth-column activities. At the time when the danger of direct German invasion of East Anglia was very imminently threatened the senior A.R.P. officers were called to consultation with the Regional Commissioner for East Anglia, Sir Will

Spens, a meeting to which it was convenient for me to go by bicycle. As I cycled quietly over the Fen from Newnham Mill Pool it was peaceful and sunny, and as I reached the river bank opposite the Garden House Hotel I was marginally aware only of a single large bird, a duck flying up from the lower stream towards the upper river and pointing directly my way, neck outstretched. I reflected idly that birds do not fly into objects, and knew no more except a hard blow of a feather-shod wing-base across the top of my nose. I came to on the macadam of the path, sitting up within the frame of my fallen bicycle, its wheels (like my head) spinning, and a large bewildered duck also slowly circling on the stream. Against all the odds I had been dive-bombed by a Muscovy duck and took a mild concussion around with me to the meeting which I followed less clearly than was proper.

Another aspect of the local alarums was the stationing, latish in the war, of the R.A.F. vehicles of the Emergency Transport Unit, an organisation for evacuation at short notice of air-fields subject to heavy attack. The presence in the black-out in winter of such a concentration of vehicles under the giant elms of the Backs made the college avenue a spooky place and when after the long walk in darkness one put one's key in the familiar gate-lock, one was likely as not to suffer confrontation by a nervous sentry fingering his unfamiliar weapon: I came to prefer the longer route by Burrell's Walk.

With the onset of heavy air-attack upon London, Cambridge of course became a reception area, and indeed at quite an early stage some of the London University components established themselves here. Thus, the Botany School was swollen by the addition of students from Bedford College and medical students came from the London Hospital when the cadavers for Professor Boyd's anatomy classes were examined in the upper floors of the Sedgwick Museum, temporarily displacing the collections of fossils used in the 'Student's series'. Dixon Boyd was with alacrity restored to his college fellowship and by living at our home, was able easily to share the pernoctation in the college

Memorial Court. As bombing disturbed their London home, Mrs Boyd and their two small boys also came to live with us, as subsequently did other old friends from their London home and successive pairs of Bedford College students who were part of the quota that Margaret, as local billeting officer, quartered upon us.

The front lawns of the college were converted to grow beans and potatoes whilst the inside walls of the Court were graced with tomatoes, and at home Dixon Boyd and I took to parallel activities, and went to the length of cultivating an allotment of the neighbouring old pasture where its high fertility and double digging yielded such surplus green vegetables that they augmented supplies to the college kitchen. The old court kitchen offered strictly limited space for servicing the augmented population and we had much reason to thank the bursar, W. J. Harrison, for skilfully negotiating an arrangement whereby the college kitchen staff undertook all cooking, whilst food rations from both college and R.A.F. sources were amalgamated. Thanks to this arrangement we were happy to escape also the no-doubt-praiseworthy sparsity for which some of our neighbour colleges took credit.

By short visits on leave the college was kept in touch, if only in a shadowy way, with the many colleagues whose scholastic expertise had made them natural recruits as 'boffins' in specialised, and often highly secret Government establishments. Thus C. W. Phillips had hardly finished the wonderful disinterment of the Anglo-Saxon ship-burial at Sutton Hoo, than he, together with almost all the staff of the University Department of Archaeology, moved into the Photographic Interpretation unit at Medmenham, where they joined that pioneer of air-reconnaissance of the First War, Dr H. Hamshaw Thomas of the Botany School Staff. Others of course swelled the miscellaneous talent of the Bletchley establishment or belonged to *ad hoc* groups bringing specialised scholastic ability to the widest range of war-problems in a pattern of response unimagined during the First World War, and, as one learned, very different in kind from that employed by the German war organisation. Naturally enough our visitors disclosed little or nothing of their work, and it was not until the War was well ended that we discovered how even at the time they had the keys to many current events in their heads. Thus I recall that in the most extensive fire-raising air-raid that Cambridge suffered, it was apparent to anyone that the great bulk of incendiaries had clustered in an area on the fringe of the built-up town, and at the foot of the Gog-Magog hills. To anyone used to assessing field-evidence, it seemed apparent that a massive systematic error was affecting the bomb-aiming. It was not until well after the War that the enthralling account of war-time Scientific Intelligence was published by R. V. Jones and offered possible explanation. It was discovered that the Luftwaffe pilots were not visually identifying the bomb targets but were utilising the projection from a home base of a remarkably narrow radio beam, down which they could fly until the interception of a cross-beam in the headphones commanded release of the bomb-load. A central course in the main beam was ensured by the pilot balancing the 'dot' signals from one flank of the beam against the 'dashes' transmitted on the other flank. With this knowledge effectively proven and the radio-frequencies determined, one is strengthened in the conjecture that in the Cambridge raid there had been distortion imposed upon the beam by our own defences. It is pleasant to think that Cambridge, Cavendish Laboratory and all, may have been saved by such means.

XVI
MEETINGS

In my undergraduate days I decided in one summer term to save the railway fare by bicycling home to the Midlands. The journey was impressive because the route crossed all the outcrops of the harder geological strata, so that I had to dismount a good deal. None-the-less, upon arrival at the level-crossing near my home, my last descent from the saddle revealed that the flannel trousers had now worn into a pair of large circular holes. At thirty shillings a pair the journey had been quite expensive.

Such thoughts recur to me when I reflect upon the enormous proportion of one's time as college don and university teacher is likewise spent wearing out the seat of one's trousers at an endless succession of meetings, conferences, discussions, supervisions and similar activities (if that is not too strong a term). Certainly from the moment that I first accepted the career of a don, I began to learn the trade of management by committee meetings: dons simply cannot help it, they so enjoy exposition that they cannot leave any meeting without benefit of explanation, even self-contradictory. There are of course differences in approach and I recall how pleasurably I discovered the contrast between the young Cambridge don and his counterpart from Oxford. In the warm excitement of chatter after a highly successful dinner in King's College, the Cambridge men, mostly scientists, first listened to their Oxford guests propounding a brilliant hypothesis, and then demolished it with exact painstaking argument: they deeply cared about the *truth* of the reasoning. It seemed that in the other place the fashion did not move thus, for the exponents of the idea, unabashed, now simply set forward another conjecture, an exercise in which the felicity of the exposition mattered more than ultimate validity.

Was this, I wondered, a consequence of P.P.E., or a more convinced preoccupation with politics?

Thanks, I suspect, to the foresight of Henry Thirkill, I did not miss the chance of election as a young research student, to that highly valued society of young men who constituted the Natural Sciences Club, and got great pleasure from the company and clear minds of many who were later to become household names in the scientific world. Our respect for the niceties of procedure was based, in intention at least, upon proper Parliamentary procedure, although we had traditions not, I believe, now active in Westminster. Thus the President would regularly during reading of the minutes, call upon the junior member to 'consume the whale', a ceremony that involved consumption of a hot sardine on toast, obligingly provided and conserved by the host of the evening before his coal fire. Much, much later, I happily became a member of the dining club for far more senior Cambridge scientists; nothing whatever would induce me to compare these two incomparable bodies, or to say to which I owed most.

My most systematic and extensive experience of university administration arose, as it must have done with many others, in the implementation of the report of the Royal Commission on the Universities of Oxford and Cambridge directly after the First World War. It provided financial support from the Government for those greatly increased costs involved by modern university teaching, more especially in the experimental sciences. Of greater importance however was the creation of a body of new statutes that changed the whole structure and relationships of university and colleges. Administration was now given a deliberately democratic structure, and one that seems to me to have been largely realised in practice. The university is headed by three senior administrative bodies of which the highest authority is the Council of the Senate that is concerned with relations between the university, Government, City and colleges. Secondly there is the Financial Board, in charge of all money matters, and thirdly the General Board which controls all teaching and research including staffing and scope. A rotational election system from categories of members of college and university is meant to secure fair and flexible representation. A similar system applies to the various categories of body operating through the General Board, notably the Faculty Boards that act in consultation with the General Board. These bodies now replace the former hegemony of professorial heads of departments and allow participation by members of staff and other concerned parties. Thanks to devoted and highly competent graduate officers in charge, the whole system, though complex, remains effective.

I must have served upon my own Faculty Board of Biology 'A', over a great many years and learned how the many experienced as well as younger members vetted all proposals for lecture courses, new posts, fresh buildings, examinations, visiting conferences and so forth: the heads of departments concerned had due but not overriding influence in reaching decisions that were transmitted to be the basis of General Board Policy. In counter-flow the senior body kept the Faculty Boards informed of impending action or were asked for advice on specific issues. Correspondingly, matters dealing with research were dealt with by the Faculty Board's own 'Degree Committee' which had a two-way contact with the University Board of Research Studies.

In what I might call mid-career I came to serve as a newly appointed Reader upon the General Board itself, serving for ten years or so and moving, under a succession of Vice-Chancellors, to increasing seniority in the body. As responsible for all teaching and research in the university it was in many respects the most powerful of the university administrative bodies and it attracted to its service men like Henry Thirkill (Master of Clare), E. C. Tilley (Senior among science Professors and eminent petrologist) and J. T. Saunders (one-time zoologist and supremely competent Secretary General of the Faculties). Under the hand of the Vice-Chancellor and supported by its graduate staff, we acquired experience in a sequence of bodies that sorted out 'straightforward business', reported on financial considerations or gave consideration to specific issues, most notably those of priority and relationship to the University Grants Committee. We regularly received and assimilated a mountain of material for preconsideration and became skilled at detecting for analysis those issues on which one could expect the Vice-Chancellor's invitation to expound. It behoves me to emphasise that during the years in which I served, I never knew the General Board do other than place in front of all other interests those of the university itself, and the slightest hint of axe-grinding from any member, great or small, closed the ranks of the rest of the body quite hermetically. I remember how one new and ambitious young man sought to satisfy his departmental head by reporting back the discussions with attributions and conclusions of the Board on issues affecting the department: this essay quickly detected by the professorial response, brought from the Board the strictest of (necessary) injunctions on cabinet secrecy. The General Board was a body with an excellent record of all-round competence and I well recall the opinion given me one evening after dinner by Sir Owen Wansborough-Jones, whom I had asked (as more likely to be able to reply than most) how difficult one would find the administrative duties if one were to take a post in the Scientific Civil Service. 'My dear Godwin' said he confidently, 'compared with the General Board, it's chicken feed.'

No doubt the exercise of power among one's colleagues has dangerous attractiveness and as I became senior and experienced in its ways, I began to feel attraction in a career as university administrator, until one or two tentative enquiries as to my possible interest in a Vice-Chancellorial post brought me up sharply. Accordingly when I became head of the Botanical Department in 1960, I decided that a door had better be open or shut, and concluded my long stint at the General Board, turning with renewed affection to the task of promoting Cambridge botany: a case indeed of 'il faut cultiver nos jardins'.

The affection which it will be apparent, was engaged in me by the work of the General Board, had been awakened, although in less extensive area and substantially sooner, by my being made a Syndic of the Cambridge University Press, where at that time Frank Kendon was Assistant Secretary, to be afterwards joined as Press Secretary by R. J. L. Kingsford of my own year in Clare but subsequently employed in the Press business in the New York and London offices. In the book-lined Syndicate Room on the Old Press site were held afternoon meetings of great precision and charm. Printed agenda before the Syndics were of substantial size, but had been predigested by the staff to a state in which the individual scholastic power of each Syndic was instantly brought to bear on the critical appraisal of each author and book, or proposal brought newly to the Press. Such was the breadth of scholarship around the table that I do not recall a failure by the Chairman directly to elicit either an immediate authoritative opinion on the author, the book and its potential, or, at the very least, effective instruction on whereabouts in the scholastic world such opinion might be found. Not uncommonly one might find oneself charged with the task of reporting to the Syndicate upon a new typescript, and if one sought to evade this duty by disclaiming special knowledge, one might very well find that one's colleagues looked on this as the precise recommendation they were seeking.

Those Syndics who had completed such a task of appraisal now reported their conclusions, not uncommonly in terms of such exactitude, fairness and wit as to constitute descriptive essays of great effectiveness. I recall the contented satisfaction with which we all settled in our chairs to listen when it was the turn of the great C. H. Dodd to summarise his reactions and conclusions. For my own part I had become a 'Press author' with the publication of *Plant Biology* in 1929, was editor of two botanical journals published by the C.U.P., and through Frank Kendon had been able to enjoy meeting and talking with that prince of University Printers, Walter Lewis.

MEETINGS

I never sat on a committee that gave me more pleasure, and more earned my respect than the Press Syndicate of those days. This was not only due to its own special composition, I believe, but reflected my own persistent pleasure in all matters associated with the publishing trade, a profession so admirably calling upon aesthetic judgment, practicality in execution and familiarity with the world of letters. The heart of it has been beautifully set out by Brooke Crutchley, himself distinguished successor to Lewis as University Printer, in his biography *To be a Printer* (1980).

When I first entered botany as a profession the tradition still survived in our British universities, as in the German ones from which they had taken so much tradition and structure, of the 'Herr Professor' as overwhelmingly powerful, with the destinies of students and staff entirely in his hand. Although this condition was altering and Seward was far from autocratic, it was certainly helpful that he approved of my botanical activities in the junior demonstratorship. The Botany School at this time was generally the most highly regarded of British botanical departments, and Seward was probably the most widely known and powerful of botanical scientists, and he was of course assuming the Presidency of the International Congress due to be held in Cambridge in 1930. The arrangements for this event, attended by a thousand visiting scientists provided abundant tasks for his staff, of whom none took half so substantial a burden as F. T. Brooks, who, as biological secretary for the British Association, was already highly experienced as organiser of large scientific meetings. As his eager off-sider I learned a vast amount of the problems of providing housing, transport, lecture-room and laboratory accommodation for so large and so varied a population already specialised into many sections. Assiduity, foresight and constant attention to detail were the hall-marks of an organisational operation much praised in its outcome, and I had much reason to remember Brooks' precepts in my own organisation of many subsequent congresses, none more demanding than the Tenth International Congress in

Edinburgh over which I had the honour of presiding in 1964. There the meeting took over four years of preparation and was attended by no fewer than 3,660 botanical scientists. It was a singularly happy chance that the General Secretary for the Congress should be Dr Harold Fletcher, Director of the Royal Botanic Garden and favourite pupil of my wife's school-teaching days.

In 1948 G. E. Briggs of St John's succeeded F. T. Brooks in the headship of the department and I was appointed Head of the newly-created Sub-department of Quaternary Research. I was responsible to the heads of those university departments most concerned to benefit from improved knowledge of the most recent of geological eras, that is to say geology, geography, biology and archaeology. These were the sciences that had backed my proposal, made to the university as early as 1938. I retained laboratory space in the Botany School and research assistance was provided by the General Board and by various learned bodies to whom suitable applications were made. My own college likewise helped very greatly in providing accommodation for the small international groups of leaders of research invited to prosecute common interests and examine problems of current interest. A common room generously stocked with refreshments enabled friendships to be developed and research projects to be ripened and happily Clare came to have a much appreciated role in befriending Quaternary studies, so much so in later years that invitations to attend were actively sought, not necessarily always from those most invitable.

Whilst dwelling so much upon one's experience of university affairs and university administration, it is only fair to recall the autonomy and ancient precedence of the individual colleges and more especially so in the case of our own eminent and gifted foundress, Elizabetha de Clare, whose mid-fourteenth-century Statutes she drafted herself to achieve her own clearly-envisaged social purposes. Her provisions were of such quality that they entered substantially into the drafting of many later colleges in both Oxford and Cambridge and remain the backbone of our present governance, a matter it seems to me, offering satisfaction to the women students and fellows who have, since 1972, become part of the college. Those early statutes foresaw most of the problems of maintaining a self-governing academic society and laid down especially useful and exact instructions upon procedure when the mastership of the college should become vacant. I have now four times experienced this process, latterly as senior fellow to whom the duties of initiation and control are given by statute. Every such election involves a sequence of meetings of the fellows, naturally interspersed with a good many informal discussions and regroupings as opinions shape and alter as to possible choice. It is naturally in the college interest that such discussion be kept within college walls. The account given by Lord Snow in his book *The Masters* has naturally been taken to owe a good deal to events in his own college: it has so authoritative a complexion that it is perhaps too readily taken as the common pattern of a college mastership election. My own reaction is to emphasise how greatly one election differs from another, in one instance choice being instant and unopposed and in another provoking endless coming and going.

It has to be recollected that as the decades pass the needs (and advantages) of the mastership alter, as do the views of the fellows, responding as they must, to ever-changing social conditions and concepts. From affording the rare opportunity of marriage within the college society, membership of a terribly select society of 'Heads of Houses' and duties light enough to allow pursuit of scholastic studies undiminished, it has become one more of the heavy new administrative posts concerned in the management of a much enlarged and very active body of fellows, scholars and commoners. Ability and even familiarity with university and national committee work increasingly are thought of as advantageous, and now that it is no longer obligatory to limit one's choice to Oxford or Cambridge M.A.'s, steps are increasingly taken to review a wider circle of choice that now embraces big business, the high ranks of the Civil Service and the armed forces. Some of the possible choices in these professions are apt, one finds, to regard a college master-ship as demanding less than full-time service or even full residence, an attitude that encourages in the fellows recon-sideration of the more generous and whole-hearted devotion they could expect from, shall we say, a tutor whose previous service and enthusiasm is beyond question and whose popularity with former members of the college is well known.

If one bears in mind these many considerations and recalls that tides of political and sociological fashion sweep through college bodies as they do through the nation, it will be apparent that choice of a new master is inevitably hard to forecast. Those who have to make the choice moreover, do not spend their time exclusively on the problem (as possibly Snow's account suggests) but for the main part revert to the tasks of scholarship in which their expertise and steady good sense are readily recognisable.

XVII
PUBLIC COMMITMENTS

A GREAT DEAL of public attention has in the last few years been directed to the wide extension of interest and belief in communism that took place in the 1930s among the brighter circles of scholarship in Cambridge. Much of the movement has been readily identified with the activity of young economists, notably Maurice Dobb, and of course with the exclusive 'Apostles' society, source of several notorious defectors.

These activities came only marginally to the notice of young scientists heavily preoccupied with their own research work so that they were not actively aware of a great revolution quietly in progress throughout the Marxist world. This amounted to the fact that it had now become standard practice and indeed orthodox policy, that all scientific research in the U.S.S.R. must be subject to central control in the presumed best interests (primarily economic and material) of the state. It is hard, a half-century afterwards, to realise with what enthusiasm this new doctrine was embraced by young Cambridge (indeed British) scientists, but it was heavily publicised and recommended by such outstanding scholars and convincing speakers as J. B. S. Haldane, J. G. Crowther, J. D. Bernal and Josiah Stamp. Important scientific organisations, such as the Association of Scientific Workers and sections of the British Association, along with journals as influential as *Nature* brought a great convergence of pressures for the introduction in this country also of central planning of all scientific administration, a frame of mind encouraged by the necessity of war-time organisation of science and scientists. Tremendous influence in this direction was exercised by J. D. Bernal's book, *The Social Function of Science* published in 1939. Professor M. Polanyi has summarised the Marxist doctrine as depending on the notion that the progress of science occurs in response to practical needs, that there is no essential distinction between science and technology and that therefore all scientific research ought to be organised with practical aims in mind. Finally all research, scientific or technical, ought accordingly to come under central direction as part of planning the national economy.

Pure science was derided and compared by Bernal with the solution of cross-word puzzles; the Soviet Ambassador told a meeting in London 'We in the Soviet Union never believed in pure science', and it was evident that freedom for independent scientific research and expression were gravely threatened. Happily there were clear and unbending minds who recognised the threat, though they were tardily supported. Most prominent and constantly active among them was Dr John D. Baker, an Oxford zoologist whose outright criticism of *The Social Function of Science*, quickly drew support from the Manchester scientist and philosopher, Professor Michael Polanyi and Sir Arthur Tansley, Sherardian Professor of Botany at Oxford. They combined to found in 1941 the 'Society for Freedom in Science' and all of them wrote powerfully against the prevalent trend to totalitarianism in science, gradually gathering the support of many solid colleagues of like belief. In 1942 Tansley delivered the Herbert Spencer Lecture at Oxford upon 'The Values of Science to Humanity', which was made available for purchase, and a substantial part of which appeared in *Nature*. In it he sought to establish that science arose not only or even mainly from economic demands, but sprang directly from man's natural curiosity. Secondly he strove to convey that over and above the high benefits it confers on our material civilisation, 'it also has intellectual, ethical, aesthetic and ultimately spiritual values of a high order'.

I was happy from the start to subscribe to the Society's statement of beliefs and to help when occasion allowed in supporting the case of pure science and for freedom in science. Opportunity arose in 1948 when, through my association with both the *New Phytologist* and the Journals of the British Ecological

Society, I was brought into the discussion being then organised by the Royal Society on the subject of the central control of all scientific publication. The Society for Freedom in Science was alerted and quickly arranged to have its viewpoint represented at the meeting: I myself drafted strong criticism of the proposals being put forward: the recommendations turned upon the idea that a central organising committee would order and pay for all scientific offprints whatever, distributing them to all who enrolled to receive contributions within each carefully restricted field of research. The cost of the service (it was said) could be kept low since the reprints would be obtainable at the currently low charge to authors, whilst departments and individuals would now be freed to a large extent from the need to purchase the journals themselves. As part of the logic of rearrangement, papers for publication would go in the first instance to the 'Central Committee' who would allocate them for editing, processing and publication, to the several journals.

These proposals, despite the blatant danger of control by a Marxist power block, won a surprising measure of support from within the Royal Society at the public discussion in the lecture-theatre of the Royal Institution; but the Society for Freedom in Science was well represented among the speakers and the subject had been well-aired by the letter to *The Times* over the signature of John Baker and Professor Tansley, and by the favourable comment on this letter in *The Times*' leading article of the same day. It was made apparent, as could have been foreseen by any informed scientific publisher, that the producers of scientific journals could not financially support any such plan, even were they willing to undertake voluntarily such a large burden of unremunerative work under outside direction. Faced with the implacable consistence of this argument, the prime mover of the plan, J. D. Bernal, sensibly and at once withdrew it.

I have to admit that throughout the spread of the movement in Cambridge I always felt intense disquiet that so many young scientists with research of high quality to their credit, could so uncritically embrace the totalitarian moonshine and I was dismayed to witness their judgment thus compartmentalised. This dichotomy was nowhere more decisively pointed out than in the review, published in 1939, by Professor H. Dingle of J. D. Bernal's own statement of faith, *The Social Function of Science*. Dingle, during an extremely thorough consideration, commented upon 'one of the most fascinating enigmas of the modern scientific world, namely the mentality of Professor Bernal himself'. He rightly recognised, as did all Bernal's scientific contemporaries, the 'quality of mind, power of balanced judgment and a command of the widest fields of scientific knowledge and thought that were conspicuous among the leaders of our time'. These attributes Dingle forthrightly contrasted with Bernal's 'apparent ignorance and irresponsibility when writing of the relation of science to other departments of thought and action'.

The animal behaviourist, Lorenz, has shewn us all how his goslings, deprived of their natural parents, are subject to swift imprintation of the first available substitute as replacement. It seems inevitable that so sensitive and intelligent a child as Bernal, educated in an Irish Jesuit seminary, must have been subject to the strongest emotional impression by the father figures of the Catholic religion. Likewise upon his intellectual rejection of those religious beliefs when he adopted communism, it must have been entirely natural that the new religion would itself supply the substitute parent figure, with its attendant unconscious imprintation. It is not hard, given the initial religious conversion, to see the *Social Function of Science* as a long emotional sermon dedicated to the Marxian dialectic and aimed to convert to the Neo-Marxian theory of science those people made ready by the disillusions of war to exchange their previous religious convictions for belief in omniscient 'Big Brother'.

There were doubtless many reasons why the tide of sympathy for the 'Commissar constitution' receded from the later 1940s. The assumption that state-organised science *must* be more effective than 'free science' had always been unsupported, and now the passage of time allowed everyone to witness an open experiment. This was the so-called 'Lysenko Affair' in which for doctrinaire political reasons the great Russian geneticist, N. I. Vavilov, was displaced from his directorship of the Lenin Academy of Genetics and during the tenure of his successor, T. D. Lysenko, the science of genetics as understood throughout the western world was eliminated from the Soviet Union, to be replaced by the unsubstantiated hypotheses of acquired characteristics. Judged objectively, it was of course stupid to proscribe the practice of Mendelian genetics, which had led everywhere in the world to those instances of technological success in plant- and animal-breeding so much desired by the Russian regime. During 1942 Vavilov had been elected a Foreign Member of the Royal Society, but his disappearance shortly after his demotion, and the failure of enquiries from the Soviet Academy of Sciences as to his whereabouts and condition, led the President of the Royal Society, Sir Henry Dale, in November 1948 to tender his own resignation from the Soviet Academy.

The withdrawal of all support from the free scientists of the rest of the world had a great effect in demonstrating the impotence of dialectical theory in directing scientific research and Bernal greatly damaged his reputation by the stand he took in the controversy, not least by his reference to 'Stalin, protector of Science'.

Concern with the public and social relationships of science was not by any means solely a matter of defending the freedoms of its practitioners. From the beginning of the century there had been a gradual perception of the principles of an emergent new science, or more accurately, of a new scientific approach, that of ecology. This at first was met with great resistance, indeed derision, in large areas of plant and animal biology. However it was increasingly in tune with the growing majority of people who thought, along with Mark Twain, that 'The country is the real thing, the eternal thing, it is the thing to watch over, and care for and be loyal to; institutions are extraneous to it, they are its mere clothing, and clothing can wear out, become ragged, cease to be comfortable, cease to protect the body from winter, disease and death.' The small size of Britain and a high susceptibility induced by dense population, easier transport and flourishing industry had, before the Second World War, made conservation an important issue, the encouragement of which none-the-less was entirely in the hands of private organisations, in particular the National Trust, the Council for the Preservation of Rural England and the Society for the Promotion of Nature Reserves. In the closing stages of the Second World War and in the period of widespread depression that followed, many public bodies and societies, among them the British Ecological Society and the Society for Promotion of Nature Reserves put pressure upon the Government to give serious thought to conservation of the countryside and its heritage of natural wild life. It was a project sympathetically accepted by a government anxious to unite an electorate behind the restoration and improvement of the land for which so much had been staked and won. No one person gave more effective weight to the case for nature conservation than A. G. Tansley himself who published in 1945 an extremely compelling book *Our Heritage of Wild Nature* that addressed and convinced a very wide and influential readership of both the desirability and practicability of establishing a national organisation to preserve the aesthetic, cultural and scientific heritage of as much as possible of our countryside. When subsequently the Minister of Town and Country Planning appointed a Wild Life Conservation Special Committee under Sir Arthur Hobhouse, Professor Tansley was Vice-chairman, and in the absence of the Chairman through illness, had a very large part in shaping the final report, a task facilitated by the fact that the drafting secretary was a naturalist of wide experience, Cyril Diver, who had been clerk to the House of Commons. It was in no small part due to the activities of this committee that in March 1949, the Royal Charter was granted by H.M. King George VI for the foundation of the

Nature Conservancy. I remember how deeply impressed I was, as one of the party of satisfied recipients, to be handed the charter bearing the Great Seal.

The new body was created to 'provide scientific advice on the conservation and control of the natural flora and fauna of Great Britain; to establish, maintain and manage Nature Reserves in Great Britain, including the maintenance of physical features of scientific interest; and to organise and develop the research and scientific services related thereto'.

It had at one time been suggested that the Conservancy might form part of the Agricultural Research Council, but there was clearly some possibility that in so powerful and extensive a pre-existing body the newcomer might fail to command the conditions requisite for quick establishment and growth. Instead, it happily became an autonomous body receiving a block grant from the Treasury, working under a Committee of the Privy Council and responsible to the Lord President. It was thus parallel in status to the other Research Councils, the Department of Scientific and Industrial Research, the Medical Research Council and the Agricultural Research Council, fully established bodies of the highest international reputation. In December of the same year parliamentary assent was also given to the National Parks and Access to the Countryside Act.

The first chairman of the Conservancy, as was most fitting, was Sir Arthur Tansley, and Cyril Diver was its first Director General. It was they who established the primary structure of the new organisation with its eighteen members, headquarters in London and Edinburgh, and very soon thereafter, as need and opportunity arose, research stations devoted to particular areas of applied ecology and the first field-stations set in areas of outstanding conservational need. The Conservancy of eighteen members was its executive body operating through territorial committees for England, Scotland and Wales together with a powerful Scientific Policy Committee and a Finance Committee. The volume and intensity of informed assistance put at the service of the new organisation bore witness to the very wide enthusiasm for its activities. In these days when 'Quango' is a term of objurgation, it should be said that a large and solid part of the work of the Conservancy was carried out by highly qualified university scientists and public personalities who spent a great deal of time and thought working on behalf of the growing body, and claiming in return no more than the bare cost of their travel. The services of professors, fellows of the Royal Society, Lords-Lieutenant and chairmen of national bodies freely given on these terms makes a quango a bargain greatly to be valued. From the assemblages of such able and congenial colleagues I learned a very great deal throughout my association with the Conservancy through the next twenty years, a period during which it became recognised all over the world as exemplary.

In all its various fields of responsibility it had formidable problems to solve. National Nature Reserves central to its purposes were infinitely variable in size and character, substantially different between northern and southern Britain, and liable to become available at times out of kilter with resources. Some aimed to conserve specially rare species of animals and plants, some sought to preserve naturally regenerating assemblages of plant and animal life and others were key localities for geological science. Pressure to conserve varied of course, there being outstanding lists of demands from the enquiries that had preceded our establishment. Acquisition was attained by direct purchase from the limited funds or by management agreement reached with owners of sympathetic mind. It took little time for the realisation that it is far from sufficient merely to fence in an area and leave it alone. The natural processes of vegetational change and habitat alteration change the status quo, and many sites must have a degree of the management which has shaped their character, be it drainage, coppicing, sheep- or cattle-grazing or, in some instances, protection against overvisitation. By 1951 the first National Nature Reserve had been declared. This was at Beinn Eighe in Ross-shire, to be joined by large, but not excessive numbers in following years.

Naturally enough, acquisition met difficulties of competition for land, from agriculture, forestry, the armed forces and the exploitation of gravel and limestone resources. We were obviously a target for the charges of 'sterilising land' and of 'harbouring pests', but by and large objections gave way before a consistent good-neighbour policy and strongly apparent public sympathy for the Conservancy's aims.

It was a charge upon the Conservancy from the beginning to develop research and associated scientific services, and my own proclivities brought me especially into touch with the organisation of the scientific staff requisite not only for management of the reserves but for provision of advice to the Government when it was faced by such basic ecological issues as for instance, the use of weed-killers on roadside verges, the progress and consequences of myxomatosis, that first attacked our rabbit population in 1953, and the fouling of coastal waters by spillage of fuel oil. There was at first some apparent conflict between the desire of staff to embark upon 'pure' ecological research as against research supporting conservation technique, but in practice it was found highly rewarding for close contact to be kept between both aims, a feature commended subsequently by reports upon the progress of the organisation. At first there was difficulty in recruiting at the higher scientific grades, a consequence no doubt of the previous lack of employment outlet in applied ecology. The need was evident to produce a generation of good trained ecological scientists, and to this end the Conservancy, like the other Research Councils, supported a policy of giving yearly a number of research-training studentships under suitable direction in universities and similar institutions. There were also available research grants aimed to resolve specific problems.

It is by no means my purpose to attempt a history of the Nature Conservancy as it grew, enjoyed the enthusiastic labour of changing membership and staff, and adjusted to modified status, and to some degree modified function, in the governmental organisation, wherein it has now become the Nature

Conservancy Council. It occupied a great deal of my interest and energies through the years, but I was never in doubt as to its importance or ultimate success.

The interest in ecology that so much involved me with the early days of the Nature Conservancy, had the far earlier consequence of involvement with the British Ecological Society, into which I was pitchforked by A. G. Tansley in 1932, accepting together membership and the secretary's job. Thereafter I was secretary for six years and joint secretary for another eight, thence taking on editorship of the *Journal of Ecology* singly for five years and jointly for an additional three. Somehow the 1943 Presidency fitted into this long spell of service during which a great deal of attendance at meetings outside Cambridge was required: many were in London but others were based at universities throughout the country and many were organised as field-meetings. Early in this long spell of years the financial success of the *Journal of Ecology* allowed the Society the protective cover from which to launch the *Journal of Animal Ecology* that, under the inspiring leadership of Charles Elton, very soon grew to independence. By 190 the membership of the Society had risen above 1,000 and both journals commanded high international reputations.

It would be fair to comment that in living so closely with the affairs of the British Ecological Society and helping to foster the movement for a national conservation service in Britain, we had been privileged to have a ring-side seat at the world-wide movement for the approbation of ecological attitudes and objectives. I hope it is not unfair in this context to employ a popular phrase and add that I enjoyed a pleasurable and close contact with the 'grass-roots' of the movement in my association with the earliest days of the founding of the 'Council for the Promotion of Field Studies' that afterwards became the Field Studies Council.

In the later part of the War Francis H. C. Butler, in his work as H.M. Inspector of Schools, had been deeply impressed by the need for facilities to help the very numerous folk, but especially school children, who were excited by the wonder of the world of wild life and all agog to investigate it for themselves. Cambridge was a convenient centre for discussion and Francis Butler brought many of us, but especially Tansley and myself, into plans to give reality to his ideas for means of encouraging every kind of field observation and research. Butler's blazing enthusiasm for a case that was inherently appealing, led to strong response for the proposal to set up a series of Field Centres at which studies could be undertaken over long or short periods of residence, within the areas of archaeology, botany, geography, geology, and zoology, all with a variety of local emphasis.

The Council was founded in 1943, and as I had been involved with the early meetings at which organisation was determined and staff chosen, it was perhaps unsurprising that I was asked to be chairman of the management committee for one of the first Field Centres, that at Flatford Mill, East Bergholt. It was extremely appealing to be thus involved with the former home of John Constable, and to help revitalise a sector of the English countryside of such significance. The Flatford Mill project had from the outset the enormous asset of the wardenship being undertaken by E. A. R. Ennion, the well-known artist illustrator of the bird-life of the Cambridge-shire fens, who indeed gave up his medical practice at Burwell and came with his family to live at Flatford. Whilst they waited for their own accommodation to be finished in the mill-house, Eric lived in a caravan on the site, playing a most active role in organising and furnishing the dormitories, refectories and laboratories in the mill itself. It all proved a thoroughly successful pioneer venture, the Ennions' warm personality and knowledge of wild nature attracted large numbers of student classes, and by a stroke of genius Eric arranged for the talented professional painter, Anthony Devas, to come up to give art-classes and to sponsor a scheme for a few art-students to come into residence alongside the larger numbers of young biologists. Margaret and I found great satisfaction in visiting Flatford for the necessary meetings, we were refreshed by the humming and eager activity of the Mill's occupants, by the sight of Willy Lott's cottage across the Mill Pool and by the scent of the spices being ground in the tide-mill downstream on the Stour. By 1960 no less than six similar Field Study Centres were operative in various parts of Britain, sited in different types of countryside. They have remained conspicuously successful and are a great tribute to the perspicuity and persistence of Francis Butler and the many enthusiasts who have followed his lead.

Flatford Mill. John Constable's mill at East Bergholt, now adapted as a Field Study Centre

XVIII
RESEARCH ADOPTED

THE PIONEER ACTIVITIES of the Fenland Research Committee had made many of us aware of the significance of
Quaternary Research, i.e. the discovery of what happened in
this country and elsewhere from the time when the first ice-sheets
began to invade temperate Europe to the time when historical
records effectively begin. We had seen how readily and fruitfully
scientists could combine the results of their various disciplines
to reach common understanding of the particular events and
places concerned. Thus, towards the end of 1938 the three
University Faculty Boards of Biology 'A', of Archaeology and
Anthropology and of Geography and Geology gave support to
a memorandum for the General Board in which I urged
proposals for encouraging Quaternary studies. It was not
altogether surprising that the financial stringency then pre-
vailing and the prospect of war should have made shelving of
the scheme inevitable.

When however in 1943 the university, following the line of
Government policy, asked for a specific statement of post-war
needs, similar suggestions were reiterated for establishing a
university body or institution to be primarily concerned with
Quaternary Research. The project adopted after the lapse of
five years by the General Board resulted in the creation of a
Sub-department of which I was made Director, responsible in
the direction of research to the heads of the Departments of
Botany, of Archaeology and Anthropology and of Geology. A
readership now secured for me a professorial level of income and
excluded me from undergraduate supervision so that I now
could devote my energies substantially to building up the new
organisation. It might perhaps be thought that my election to
the Royal Society in 1945 had lent wings to the proposal and

secured some advantage in the never-ceasing competition for assistance. Research students from various parts of the world came to share the experience of the Sub-department and we were provided with research assistants and technicians as funds could be found. As time went on we made increasingly close contact with research workers in the Quaternary of western Europe and North America, visits took place in both directions, and we ensured a flow of information not only by the circulation of reprints of scientific papers but also by the issue annually of a detailed report of all we were doing.

It would be inappropriate to catalogue the very various activities that were now engaged upon, and I will mention our major preoccupations only. Pollen-analysis continued to play a large part in all the research since it gave us the quasi-chronological basis for most enquiries. We continued to exploit the richness in archaeological and stratigraphic evidence from the relict peat-bogs of the Somerset Levels, most particularly the elaborate wooden trackways that we were able to refer to their Neolithic and Bronze Age horizons, and the evidence for flooding horizons affecting the great raised bogs and for sea-level changes modifying the inland incursion of marine deposits.

We now began to be able to recognise and date the so-called 'Late-glacial' period, when the last stages of glaciation shewed withdrawal and melting of the British ice sheets, albeit with typical temporary reversal. The evidence came from as far south as the kaolin workings in Cornwall and the Lea Valley just north of London, but was also unmistakably recognised in the bottom deposits of Windermere. Before long it was also to be demonstrated as an essential component of the classic studies of the Mesolithic culture at Star Carr in the former Lake Pickering, between the Wolds and the Moors of north-eastern Yorkshire. Pollen-analyses shewed how the generally tree-less landscape was gradually clothed with woodland as climate ameliorated. Remains of red-deer were very abundant and supplied the basis of a hunting economy and a highly characteristic industry of making the notched bone-points found with this culture all round the North Sea basin. This research represented extremely successful cooperation between different disciplines, especially centering upon the work of archaeologists organised from Cambridge by Dr Grahame Clark: the compendium in which the results were published by the University Press in 1954 still remains a classic study, *Star Carr*.

The attention of the Sub-department also focussed upon recognising and defining the long mild climatic 'Interglacial' periods that intervened between successive glaciations of this country. Organic deposits of this age were left here and there at the margins of maximum ice extension, as in Cambridge itself, in shore exposures at Clacton-on-Sea, and especially at the Hoxne brickworks in Essex. Pollen-analyses in time revealed the course of a long vegetational history reflecting rise of temperature to a thermal maximum and decline to the starkness of returning glaciation. It became possible to characterise the different interglacials individually and to acknowledge the probability that the 'Post-glacial' time in which we live at present is indeed simply the latest mild interglacial, as yet only part way through its gradual and fluctuating return to the next visitation of an Ice Age. The progress made in this field began when S. E. Hollingworth, later Professor of Geology at University College, London, was engaged in his post on the Geological Survey upon re-survey of the Cambridge–Fenland margin. He presented us with sub-fossil plant material taken from exposures in the Histon Road, Cambridge; and from the identification of fruits and seeds we recognised an interglacial origin that was confirmed and defined later on as pollen-studies yielded an historical view of vegetational events. Exciting as these early excursions into the nature of the interglacials were, the really massive impetus of exploration lay with the research of R. G. West, my successor in the Directorship of the Sub-department. He began research under my direction in 1951/2, a time when I was preoccupied by no less than three visits to the operating theatre for the removal of an ischio-rectal abscess: the reports of his competent field research brightened my hospitalisation and convalescence. My doctor confined me to house and garden whilst the weeks of healing passed, and expressed concern that I might perhaps be *bored*: I reflected that this at least was an affliction not so far affecting me, and embarked seriously on a project that was tolerable when sitting on a generous posterior packing of gauze and cotton-wool. The task was to complete and organise a card-index of all datable records of Pleistocene plant-material. Collaterally with the many pollen-analytic studies, we had, over the years, kept and identified the large plant fragments such as wood, charcoal, leaves, bud-scales, hairs, stamens and even whole flowers. To the index were now added all such identifications, and those from colleagues' publications, as were tied to indices of age, for instance stratigraphic level, pollen-analytic zone, climatic phase or archaeological culture. Each day of my recuperation saw my secretary bring me a small pack of filled-in index cards, which we worked at together. I compiled a critical statement of the history of the plant genus or species represented, using the evenings to complete reference to literature and drafting. Thus we began the assimilation of some hundreds of records which supplied a need never before realised, the factual proof that individual plant species had been formerly growing at known places and proven times within this country. It was an exercise in setting land-marks in what hitherto was a sea of biogeographic conjecture, and was the foundation of my definitive book *The History of the British Flora* that the Cambridge University Press published in 1956. It had a very approving welcome, and before long the contributions were so extensive that they were transferred to a redesigned punch-card for use with a mechanical sorting machine, the use of which made possible the publication of a second edition of the book (1975) and continued employment of the 'data bank' that is freely consulted by Quaternary research workers and botanists in this and in other countries. What had really begun as an intuitive exercise in the conservation of incidental data, and had flourished as a therapeutic exercise, turned out on adequate assimilation thus to have very worthwhile scientific value. It was quite certain that it played a part in the award to me in 1966 of the Linnaean Society's Gold Medal. In 1951 I had been honoured to receive also the Prestwich Medal of the Geological Society of London, a memorial to one of the great pioneers of Quaternary Geology. The celebratory dinner in the Tallow-chandler's Hall also has its stamp of association with my surgical experiences, for I recall sitting throughout the car-ride from Cambridge and the splendid meal upon my protective posterior packing, blessing the sympathetic surgeon who had allowed the participation.

It was a measure of the esteem which the Sub-department attracted that when Willard F. Libby, later to be made Nobel Laureate for his development of radiocarbon dating, sought in 1949 to test the validity of his method, he asked if we could supply him with samples of ancient organic material, whose age we had already determined by the methods of interlocking chronologies of pollen-analysis, stratigraphy and so forth. A swift field excursion to known sites and selection of stored samples allowed us to send a small number of our most dependable items to the Chicago laboratory, from which Libby's earliest datings emerged at a symposium of the Cambridge Philosophical Society in the following year, demonstrating a degree of correspondence with expectation that was highly satisfactory, and that was confirmed fully in the book *Radiocarbon Dating* published by Libby in Chicago, 1952.

So powerful an aid to Quaternary investigations could not be disregarded, and after a year wasted on what proved an impracticable new technique, we took advantage of the suggestion by the university's Assistant Director of Radio-chemistry, Dr A. G. Maddock, that we might attempt the method of gas-proportional counting, and that we might seek the necessary finance from the Nuffield Foundation. We had only a week in which to apply, but in hardly longer than this we had been given a five-year grant. Dr Maddock became our fairy-godmother and upon his advice we appointed a London graduate, E. H. Willis as research assistant: in next to no time all three of us were in Copenhagen, visiting the dating laboratory being operated by Dr Hilda Levi, a pupil of Nils Bohr. So began a tradition of helpful cooperation that still persists. We had help also from Harwell and the Laboratory of the Royal Institution, at that early time the only other British team engaged in radiocarbon dating. It is hard to realise now from what a vast territory of ignorance our beginnings were made. We mercifully escaped the dangers of the direct-current power-pack (built from hearing-aid batteries) by which we secured a stable high-voltage current for our counter, but temerity in working with acetylene as the counting medium ultimately led to an explosion blowing out the laboratory window and destroying the vacuum line. These hazards were overcome, and a stream of useful datings began to issue from the laboratory, all aimed primarily in support of the Quaternary Research of the Sub-department and related needs of other university investigators. By 1955 with the help of Clare and Newnham Colleges we were able to play host to an informal conference of active research-workers in radiocarbon dating from the leading American and European laboratories.

The original laboratory accommodation in the Botany School had by 1958 inadvertently and technically become too 'hot' for us, since a visiting plant-physiologist began without notice to employ as tracers in his experiments concentrations of radioactive carbon totally swamping our own ultra-se ive and minuscule measurements. We were helped by the univ 1ty hurriedly to pick up sticks, and we moved to distal ut premises in the Station Road. Here we lacked the p te on from cosmic rays we had enjoyed beneath the Botany Sc ool building, but we were able to borrow, as an alternative shield, several tons of pure distilled zinc. This served admirably, but as the price of zinc rose on the market its value was such that we feared an armed hold-up and were much relieved when the kind owners took it back and we found ourselves able to buy in its place from St John's some tons of lead that had lost its own radioactivity through honourable ageing on the roofs of the college.

The excitement and enthusiasm of the new research organisation and the general good-will towards us were now powerfully reinforced by the new research tool set both to tasks of improvement in radiocarbon dating itself and in application to crucial issues in Quaternary Research. It would be inappropriate to give a detailed account of our activities, but particular highlights engage one's recollections irresistibly. There had long stood in the entrance to the Botany School a great slice of the trunk of a giant redwood tree, whose counted succession of growth-rings had been marked by labels of historic events from before the Norman Conquest. This ancient relict we carefully plundered, taking auger samples at regular intervals over a long age span. Dried and despatched to a number of leading laboratories, the measured carbon activities gave us evidence for the reality of past variations in the natural atmospheric content of radiocarbon: this was soon to become one of the established truths to be reckoned with in carbon dating. We also hastened to establish the radiocarbon ages of the pollen-zone boundaries in a fine series of samples from Scaleby Moss in Cumberland, a stage of great significance since pollen-zonation had hitherto afforded our only generally applicable chronology from Late-glacial time to the present. We were likewise very desirous to establish the carbon dating of those phases of the Late glacial period now recognisable in the British Isles, so that in June 1958 Eric Willis and I presented an exhibit setting out our results before a conversazione of the Royal Society. It was an occasion stamped in my memory by the sound of the bleeping from the first Russian Sputnik being broadcast via the Cambridge Mullard Observatory to the assembled guests.

I recall also with particular pleasure the involvement of the Sub-department with research into the origin of the Norfolk Broads, a project independent of our carbon dating. Its most startling outcome was the demonstration at the hands of Dr Joyce Lambert, sometime research fellow of Newnham, and associated specialists, that the broad stretches of open water beside the Norfolk rivers owed their creation to peat-cutting for fuel during the thirteenth to fifteenth centuries. The coincidence of still surviving balks of peat carrying parish and property boundaries across the broads, the existence of ecclesiastical records of purchases of vast amounts of peat, the confirmation by boring of the vertical faces of the old cuttings and a host of stratigraphic and ecological data coincided to force upon ourselves and the scholastic world a conclusion of human origin previously unexpected. There seems still to me to be a peculiar attractiveness about the sudden revelation, now so self-evident to all who sail these inland-water lakes or examine the easily available photographs of them from the air.

When the time came for me to give the Croonian Lecture during the Tercentenary Year of the Royal Society, 1960, the Sub-department had gathered so much definitive evidence that one could speak on 'Radiocarbon dating and Quaternary History in Britain'. I recall how strongly I felt this address to be a progress report in a field where accumulation of new data and modification of old were bound to advance at great speed, and this indeed has proved to be the history of subsequent carbon dating and its associated sciences.

XIX
ASSURANCE

AFTER the Second World War, Clare came once more under
the pressure affecting all the Cambridge colleges to provide
increased undergraduate accommodation within the college
buildings. As the Memorial Court had originated in commemoration of the dead of the First World War, so now, after
the substantial additions of the inter-war period, it was proposed
that resumed building should be dedicated to the fallen of the
Second World War, and we were fortunate in being still able
to engage the architect of the existing court, Sir Giles Gilbert
Scott, who, by 1950 had presented the college with his first
suggested plan. As alternative to this the building committee
turned to consider the possibility of an additional court at the
south-western corner of our site. There was however too little
width, until it occurred to us that King's College might be so
friendly as to agree to make over to Clare a contiguous narrow
strip of land from their Fellows' Garden. I wrote as Chairman
of the Building Committee and they proved extremely co-
operative, permitting us to have enough land for the architect
to design, and the college to acquire, a new court of excellent
proportion, entirely in natural relationship to the existing
buildings. So tightly designed was the existing structure of the
court, however, that one could not make an entrance through
it to the new court without sacrificing at least three sets of rooms,
and eventually we provided passage between the older and
newer court by a route round the south-west corner of the
existing court. The new court was opened in 1955 and was
unhesitatingly christened Thirkill Court. Time has approved
the architectural quality of the building, especially the serenity
of the long frontage it provides to flank the main approach to
the University Library. The local expertise of the fellows had

proved helpful especially in that Professor O. T. Jones, out-standing among field geologists, should already have been consultant for the university over the foundations of the University Library. We intended a cycle-store and drying rooms beneath our new building and feared the consequences in excavating the deep late-glacial sands and gravels of this site: fortunately this basement proved neither subject to flooding, nor liable to act like a watertight tank that might lift the building above.

Involvement in college projects of this kind alongside teaching and research in the University Department and membership of the General Board illustrate what we may call the pleasurable duality (or plurality) of a don's life. It was also apparent when it became a matter for concern that Sir Henry Thirkill would, because of age-limit, retire from the mastership in 1958, and the whole Governing Body began informal search for a succes-sor. I have already in Chapter XVI touched upon the nature of the mastership election when its procedure has become subject to rule of the statutes and under direction of the senior fellow. The many meetings, groupings and considerations of issues that ensued ended in the election of Sir Eric Ashby, Vice-Chancellor of the Queen's University, Belfast, a botanist of very wide experience and one who, like myself, had very early become convinced of the great significance of ecology. This common background made it very easy for Margaret and me to engage in a preliminary visit of introduction and explanation to the new Master and Lady Ashby in their Belfast home.

When the college elected its new master in 1958 there followed a period of about a year before he was free to come into residence and during this time it fell to me to act in his stead. This was not outstandingly difficult, for I had relieved myself of other duties in preparation for assuming the Chair of Botany in the later part of 1960. College business was also much simplified by its classification into routine matters, that could be settled out of hand, and matters of principle that needed serious consideration and were postponed against the Master's attention or were perhaps passed to a committee for discussion and preparation prior to his taking over. Since I was familiar with the fellows and in touch with the general run of college business it sufficed to visit Clare each day to consult the officers and to clear correspondence. One recognised a situation not unlike that of Gilbert's 'Mikado' where, relieved of the 'troubles of a king' one accepted that 'the pleasures they are many and the privileges great'. One such pleasure was the acceptance on behalf of the college of the gift from a devoted benefactor, the Revd R. L. Payne, of a deluxe version of a fine illustrated ornithological book, of which he had already given an only slightly less beautiful copy to the college library.

Margaret and I together received the customary invitations to lunch or dinner that circulated as a matter of custom between

Proposed new court, afterwards Thirkill Court, shewn in the appeal prospectus as viewed from the west. It was completed in 1955

heads of houses and enjoyed, one need scarcely say, meeting people from university circles that we otherwise saw little of.

Somewhat in the same category was the unexpected bonus that arose when a London exhibition had been held of the 'Treasures of Oxford', and this had evoked the reasonable response within Cambridge bosoms at the Goldsmiths' Company, that they might properly now proceed to organise a similar show of the 'Treasures of Cambridge'. Thus, along with the heads of Cambridge houses, representatives of the Fitzwilliam Museum, the University Library, various university departments, and high university officials we met in some hospitable Master's drawing room, and amicably discussed how we might best wipe the eye of the other place. We were not altogether certain of what was on offer, especially by the colleges, although it was conceded that special attention must be given, in view of our sponsorship, to the college plate. The Masters however had taken advice from the fellows and one at a time, with nicely simulated modesty, enquired whether such and such a treasure might be acceptable. They deprecatingly asked, would we care to have such gems as the first edition of *The Faerie Queene*, the autograph of Gray's 'Elegy', an autograph leaf from *A Shropshire Lad*, or such evocative items as Drake's pocket-book, a letter from John Evelyn to Pepys, or maps shewing the progress of the Spanish Armada. With these were proffered the fine items of college silver, often the founder's plate itself, and portraits of distinguished sitters by no less famous artists. It was, as may be guessed, an occasion for gracious relaxation, and in due course from it and succeeding meetings there was created a wonderfully successful Exhibition held in March and April 1959. It was part of the privilege of *locum tenens* to attend the private viewing in Goldsmiths' Hall, where in the display, items loaned by colleges were supplemented by the vast resources of the Fitzwilliam Museum and the University Library. The Whipple Museum and the Cavendish Laboratory had added items of apparatus associated with those pioneers of the development of the physical sciences, Lord Rutherford,

The Scholars' Garden and Grumbold's Bridge, viewed from the parapet
above the West Front of Clare

Looking westward over the Old Court at dormer level with the belfry and guardian cherubs from behind

J. J. Thomson and Sir James Chadwick. It was all enormously impressive, not least because of the concentration of modest but eminent guests. For one cherished instant Margaret and I came unexpectedly upon Miss Cartwright, distinguished among mathematicians, standing before the portrait of herself by Stanley Spencer, the two personalities quietly contemplating one another. For a moment we were unobserved.

The Governing Body had the great kindness to mark my period as *locum tenens* by the gift of a silver rose-bowl which was not only suitably inscribed but which had its fretted convex cover designed upon the motif of sprays of the mountain-avens. This plant, *Dryas octopetala* had a very special meaning for my historical plant-geographic research, for its Late-glacial remains had been identified as far south as the Lea Valley in Essex although today it is restricted in Britain mostly to special montane and northern habitats.

The new mastership fell at a time of far-reaching change for the universities and colleges of Oxford and Cambridge. The first great evolutionary step of the previous hundred years had been already accomplished by allowing the marriage of college fellows, and we had experienced more than twenty years' effective operation of the second change, that of the revised administrative organisation of colleges and university. Now however we were exposed to the full consequences of the whole-hearted intervention of the National Government from the late 1940s in the financing of university education. Provided that a requisite standard of entry had been reached, fees and maintenance were now provided at Oxbridge colleges for a greatly increased range of students who had hitherto been debarred by the cost. This altered the whole financial climate of many colleges, for each was now assured of filling its whole complement of places.

We had now also begun a regime in which the weight of university teaching was sustained by money coming from the University Grants Committee and the numbers of university teaching posts were greatly augmented, whilst the university to

H. G. – the author

a large extent kept its autonomy and colleges reaped indirect financial benefit since the fellows were adequately remunerated by their university posts. This financial relief permitted great expansion in the numbers elected to fellowships, elevating the bare dozen of the 1925 Clare body to several times that number. Furthermore, not only was the undergraduate intake now less preponderantly drawn from the public schools but so too, inevitably were the college fellows and the university administration.

By 1960 however the strain had become apparent of accommodating within the college fellowship system the full number of all the newly-created university teaching officers. A fellowship was apt to be regarded as one of the rights of the post, although colleges had no direct say in the appointment and the teaching was often in subjects not much needed by colleges to assist work for the Tripos examinations. There were indeed in early prospect the reports of three committees of enquiry upon the imbalances of the situation and we were soon to be familiar with recommendations under the names of the chairmen, respectively Robbins, Bridges and Franks. There were those who waved the threat of another Royal Commission should the colleges fail to accept the proposals, and for Clare, closely constricted by its lack of space in Kitchen, Combination Room and Offices within the Old Court, the occasion was one challenging to a new master of vision and experience. And over the horizon there might easily be discerned the shape of proposals that colleges should adopt co-residence of women students.

Not only in college did 1960 and thereabouts shew the character of a watershed and a prospect of change. It was in 1960 that I was elected to the University Chair of Botany thus taking administrative responsibility for a very large department, pre-eminent in its field. I recalled the considered advice of a well-known army commander that one could effectively delegate power to no more than nine people and found that this fitted our practice, which began with the University Botanic Garden under its Director, and the respective directors of the Sub-departments of Plant Physiology and of Mycology plus Plant Pathology. For the time being I continued to direct Quaternary Research. There were able senior staff who competently undertook to oversee the estimates and accounts and the management of a large staff and technical assistants. I had always held to the belief that the Professor should share elementary teaching and so become familiar and available to first year as well as advanced students, so that teaching and administration took a major portion of my time. None-the-less I soon found that one could not afford to neglect daily perusal of *The Times*, the University *Reporter* or the agenda of one's own or related Faculty Boards, together with attendance at such national or university committees as concerned the prosperity and status of one's department or staff. Busy as one was, it would be idle to pretend that this position was not after my own heart, more especially since my own interests had always embraced the whole field of botanical study and I had no desire to cocoon myself in a single specialised field. My early acquisition for the department of equipment for electron microscopy no doubt served the primary purposes of pollen-grain anatomy and so of Quaternary study, but it proved, as it was meant to do, to be of great value to many types of research going on in the building and outside.

It is somewhat odd that there does not exist in this country a Society devoted entirely to botany, taking in the whole field, now very wide indeed, of the plant sciences but not conjoined to other disciplines. This is not the case with scientific journals for there we have the *Annals of Botany* and the *New Phytologist* embracing in their scope the whole field of botanical science. The lack of a central society for all botanists gave British plant scientists a very special interest in the one world-wide organisation where botanists of every country and of every type of specialisation could meet to exchange research information, to organise common projects and formulate principles and where common action might be called for. This body takes the form of a sequence of 'International Botanical Congresses', the meetings held at intervals of four or five years in varying host-countries. Since the meeting had been held in Cambridge in 1930, as I have already recounted, I had derived very great pleasure, and not a little instruction, from attendance at

West gateway to the avenue

subsequent meetings in Stockholm and in Paris. Nevertheless it was a very great surprise to me to be invited to undertake the Presidency of the tenth such Congress for its next meeting, which had been fixed for the historic city of Edinburgh during

1964. It hardly requires to be said that when the news reached me in 1961, it presented a vista of three years of extremely intensive and careful organisation in Cambridge, Edinburgh, London and elsewhere, together with travel and constant forethought.

I do not propose to describe the very pleasurable progress of the Congress in 'auld reekie', but cite it now to give support to my determination that 1960 was indeed a watershed in my introduction to life as a botanist and don, and a date at which I might reasonably break off from my recollections.

ENVOI

In February 1931, I received from York a letter that I have cherished through the years: from it I take leave to copy now a few paragraphs that serve not only as a heartening reminder of an old friendship but as an illustration of the faith on which a don's life, perhaps one should say 'a scientist's life' is based. The letter was written by Nigel Balchin, a young graduate of great wit and talent whom I had supervised for his three years of undergraduate study in Peterhouse: I have written concerning him in Chapter VIII. The letter now quoted followed his secondment to a post, then rather unusual, of 'industrial psychologist'. He had been sent to Rowntrees, the chocolate manufacturers, as off-sider to a senior colleague but, when his instructor was shortly taken away, Nigel was left in sole charge of the investigations, his first adventure into business life. The letter begins with much friendly gossip and continues:

'I long to see you and Margaret in your new abode. Does M.G. still provide the kindest of damp shoulders for repressed undergraduates to cry their hearts out on? (syntax). I think you both ought to be paid a large salary as Official Cheerers-up of Depressed Youth, Also as University Seers of the Point of View of People who Really Haven't Got One.'

'...Well, I think I can fairly say, without boasting more than usual, that this job has gone quite well: certainly I have had a lot of nice things said about it, both to me directly, and indirectly through my directors. And when I was thinking it over to-day, it struck me how largely the thing is due to you and to Margaret. It has simply been a question of keeping it detached, and refusing to have any preconceived ideas about it. One of the directors here put it in a nutshell when he said to our director "The reason why your man has managed to do what our own staff could not is, that coming to the job fresh, he has always refused to accept the ideas, even of the most experienced of us, unless we could show some facts to support them." Well, H.G., I don't want you to think I have set the Thames on fire, but I appreciated that, because I know that is what I aimed to do, and I know it is what you would do in the circumstances. I may not be a particularly straight thinker, but I do realise that if it had not been for you I should have been even more cork-screwlike, and I want you to know how much I appreciate it. It is an immense relief to find that the good people in industrial jobs are not so very much better than oneself, and that the good old style of deduction from fact will work whether one is packing chocolates or doing ecology.'

Nigel's letter appeals to me especially because it confirms that from my earliest contacts with students I had an overriding belief in the need for truthfulness in argument with them and indeed took intellectual honesty as a simple necessity for both teacher and scholar. It was this belief that brought me from school to Cambridge and in college and scientific laboratory ensured the massive friendship of so many amiable and admirable scholars and colleagues. Once admitted to the society of scholars there is no limit to the helpfulness they will display in helping one forward: however young and inexperienced one may be, one will receive direct encouragement. It has been my immense good fortune to have encountered in school, college and university such consistent support that this book could well have been entitled 'The helpfulness of Scholars'. In any event I intend that it shall express my recollection of, and gratitude towards, those many eminent and kindly friends who so pervasively directed one's pursuits.

It was evident that whether one's aim was the guidance of students or the process of one's own self-instruction by reading and research, no principle takes precedence over that of intellectual honesty, and that the handmaidens of such activities are clarity of thought and lucidity of expression, virtues which, after all amount to very much the same thing. Whether the doctrine persists I do not know, but there used to be a favoured view among psychologists that thought was only possible through the formulation of words.

Once the rigour of honest reasoning is agreed it is apparent
that cheating in this regard is inexcusable, either to pretend one
knows when one does not, or to refuse, after proper consideration, to accept what one knows is perceived truth. I felt as a
student, and still feel that to fail in these beliefs is inevitably the
sin against the Holy Ghost, the habit that will destroy one's own
integrity, as well as that of others. A very important part of the
virtue of Nigel Balchin lay in his several books in which his
characters, scientists and psychologists mostly, struggled to
achieve the courage to acknowledge 'Lord, I was afraid' or
merely 'I do not know', when these were the true answers.

To aim for clarity of thought and communication is all very
well, but requires the mastery of language, both read and
written, if not also spoken. Here also I was singularly favoured,
although I lacked the great advantage of classical languages
save a very modest Latin requirement. From Samuel Clegg,
incomparable headmaster, I gained familiarity with and affection for the great English writers, and remained from the age
of twelve to eighteen in his own classes and taking the London
University examinations in English, greatest of all living languages. Samuel Clegg helped my first tentative editorial en-
deavours and revised the first book I wrote and I recall that
when I had written my early text-book on *Plant Biology*
F. F. Blackman, my supervisor in research, replied to my
expression of thanks to him that 'he had beneficially criticised'
the manuscript, a remark of typical crispness and modesty. Sir
Albert Seward wrote with great facility and helped me greatly,
though never imparting his own gift of resuming writing
instantly after even the most tiresome interruption. In my years
as baby fellow in Clare I had much to do with 'Manny' Forbes,
then in the throes of writing the vast commemorative *Book of
Clare*: I was recruited to the writing of minor parts and soon
learned to appreciate the complex allusive and witty style of the
editor who currently played such an appreciated, if idiosyncratic, role in the teaching of university studies in English. To
none of these writers however, did I owe more than to Sir

ENVOI

Arthur Tansley, whose gifts as author and editor were altogether outstanding in the contribution to a wide field of biological sciences.

Although I make this special recognition of the writers as illustrative of 'The Helpfulness of Scholars' the generosity came, as it still does, from all categories of colleagues, through my time as Tripos candidate, research student, fellow of Clare and university teacher in the Department of Botany. To recount the contacts thus made has allowed me to express my admiration and gratitude, whilst helping to preserve many of the more revealing miscellanea of Cambridge academic life, and to recreate one's vision of the loveliest of Cambridge colleges.

INDEX

INDEX

Drawing and Design (by S. Clegg), 7
Dutch elm disease, 82, 87

Eastern General Hospital, 79
Easton, Hugh, 110
ecology, 9, 35, 42, 45, 50, 132,
    146–158 *passim*, 171, 195–202
    passim, 212
Ecology, Journal of, 42
Elborn, Henry (Snr.), 57–59
Elton, C., 200
Ennion, E. A. R., 201
Erdtman, G., 155, 157
Ethelbert White, 133
Evans, A. H., 94

Falcon Cup, 116
Fenland Research Committee, 157,
    174–6
Festival Theatre, 123
field-courses, 46
Field Study Centres, 200ff, *202*
Finella, 106, 112, *124*, *126*ff, 133
Flatford Mill, 200f, *202*
Fletcher, H., 188
Forbes, Mansfield Duval ('Manny'),
    13ff, 22, 30, *66*, 69, 76, 95, *96*,
    98–106, 123, 129f, 132f, 142,
    162, 225
Fowler, Gordon, 174
Freud, Sigmund, 56, 150ff
Frost, A. C., 130
Frostlake Cottage, 133
Fulford, Revd., W. H. ('Fluffy'), 68f

Galer, A. G. and Mrs Galer, 120
Gardiner, W., 58f
General Board of the University, 73,
    184ff
'Genesis', 127f
geology, 9, 16, 35, 47f
Gilbert-Carter, H., 52, 54, 162f
Gilbert-Scott, Sir Giles, 65, *66*, 78,
    89, 143, 211
Gilmour, J. S. L., 82, 94
Ginkgo biloba, 161
Gow, A. S. F., 178
Greenwood, J. F., 22, *99–103*
'Greene Cups', 120

Haldane, J. B. S., 191

'Half-moon', 122
Hall, Edward, 33
Harnshaw Thomas, H., 54, 180
Harrison, W. J., *66*f, 72, 140, *144*f, 180
'Helpfulness of Scholars', 224ff
Henderson, Hubert D., 30, *66*
Hill, R. H., 119f
History of the British Flora, 206f
Hobhouse, Sir Arthur, 196
Hollingworth, S. E., 205
Holttum, R. E., 48
Hutton, R. S., 119f
Huxley, Sir Thomas, H., 166

International Botanical Congress,
    132, 152, 187f, 220ff

James, W. O., 153
Johnston, Edward, 6
Jones, E. Alfred, 95
Jones, O. T., 156, 212
Jones, R. V., 181
Journal of Ecology, 148, 151, 200

Kendon, F. H., 79f, 186
Kerner and Oliver (*Natural History of
    Plants*), 9
Keynes, Sir Geoffrey, 173
Kidd, F., 165
Kingsford, R. J. L., 186

Lackland, 122
Lady Clare Magazine, 130ff
Lamb, C. G., 94
Lamb, H., 142f
Lambert, Joyce, 209f
Landon, W. J., *66*, 74
Lewis, Walter, 186f
Lewisite, 93f, 177
Libby, Willard R., 207
'limiting factors', 63
Little St Mary's Lane, 121ff
Lindquist, B., 133
lodgings, 20, 35, 77
Long Eaton, 1, 7
Lysenko, T. D., 195

Maddock, A. G., 207
malaria, 28
Maltby, S., 33
marriage of fellows, 19, 189, 217

228

INDEX

INDEX

supervisor, 35, 71, 81ff
Sutton Hoo, 180
Swinnerton, H. H., 16, 156

Tansley, Sir Arthur G., 43, 50, 56,
  62f, 132, 146–158, *147*, 165, 172,
  192f, 196f, 225f
Taylor, H. M., 134
teleology, 9, 63
Telfer, Revd. W., 29, *31*, 73, 100,
  123ff, 131, 140, *144*f
Thirkill, Sir H. (Master), 29–*31*, 41,
  66, 73, 76, 134–45, 141, *144*,
  183f, 212
Thomson, Sir Joseph J., 41, 135, 139,
  217
Tilley, E. C., 184
Tomlinson, H. M., 110
'Treasures of Cambridge', 214
Turner, Miss Jennie, 166
Turner, J. S., 82f

University Library, 74
  Press Syndicate, 186f

Vaerwyck, Mlle Rosa, 5

Vavilor, N. I., 195

Wadham, Sir Samuel M., 51, 54, 146
Walton, J., 54
Wane, F. I., 120
Wansborough-Jones, Sir Owen, 185
Warburton, C., 97f
Wardale, J. R., 29, *66*–69, 120
Warwick, J., 119
Webb, William (Master), 67
West, Cyril, 165
West, Gilbert, 38f
West, R. G., 39, 205
Whitby, Sir Lionel, 140
Whittaker, John, 90
Wicker Fen, 62, 94, 132, 146ff,
  148–50, 157
Widdows, G. W., 3
Willis, E. H., 208f
Willis, J. C., 163f
Wilson, G. H. A. (Master), 34f, *66*,
  71–3, 86, 95, 103–5, 131, 140
wood-block printing, 6, 79f, 130
Wootton, H. A., 93
World War, First: return from,
  17–21